Nature's Reach

Coping With Grief the Natural Way

John Allen

Table of Contents

Heavenly Father, I want to thank *you* for my countless blessings. I thank *you*, not only for the food I have to eat or the comfortable place I have to live, but for the beauty that surrounds me. I acknowledge *you* for the countless blessings that *you* have provided and continue to provide. I thank *you* for giving me clear direction through *your* Holy Word. Through the good and the bad times, I thank *you* for this life. Amen.

"But ask the animals, and they will teach you, or the birds in the sky and they will tell you; or speak to the earth, and it will teach you, or let the fish in the sea inform you. Which of all these does not know that the hand of the LORD has done this? In his hand is the life of every creature and the breath of all mankind." –Job 12:7-10

Introduction

- Are you struggling to get through the day because your grief is holding you hostage?

- Do you find yourself hiding between the layers of the cloak of grief?

- Are you afraid to stray too far from the cloak of grief for fear of forgetting your loved ones?

I believe that it is safe to assume that you have answered yes to my three questions. I also believe that this is something that everyone has gone through, and will go through, at some stage during their lifetime. You will know, if you have been following my journey, that I am struggling to come to terms with the passing of my dad. His passing has presented me with many questions which I do believe are gifts from him. Dad knew I had a love for writing, but I never knew in which direction I wanted to go, or what subjects I wanted to write about. One of my previous books—*Life After This: 9 Chapters: History Shows We Have Contacted the Deceased and You Can Do It, Too*—is an insight into why I say that Dad's passing was a gift from him. It was as if he was permitting me to share our life with millions of people who need to find their peace.

No two people will have the same experience when it comes to the loss of a loved one, or the way that they find healing. This is something I will share throughout our time together, because it is something that everyone needs to hear, see, and understand. Each person that walks about on this earth will have a different story to tell. You may be grieving differently than someone else, but it doesn't mean you are not feeling pain. Grieving is not a board game, and it is most definitely not an action game that you play online. Another of my books—*Keep Calm and Cope With Grief: 9 Chapters for Managing Fear and Grief When Losing a Parent or Loved One*—will give you an insight into the various levels of grief people experience.

All About Me

I had a Mum and a Dad who raised me to always be conscientious of other people's feelings and circumstances. They taught me that it didn't take much effort, or any of my pocket money, to be helpful, kind, caring, and polite to others. Mum and Dad taught me that doing good was the right way to live one's life. Today, I can share my experiences with the world because I was, and still am, surrounded by a loving and caring family which includes Mum, Jessica, Gillian, Alison, aunts, uncles, cousins, and close friends.

I was born and raised in the working-class city of Liverpool in the United Kingdom in the late 1960s. I can remember when friends, family, and acquaintances used to comment that I always seemed to be on a different planet. Some would say that I was a deep thinker, and others would say that I would think before I acted. Everyone would be right with their assumptions, but what nobody knew was that I was always thinking about the future. I remember sitting on the windowsill in my bedroom as an eight- or nine-year-old boy. We didn't have distractions such as gaming consoles, computers, or devices that could influence our way of thinking back then. I had a crystal-clear view of my backyard, and a bird's-eye view of what was going on in my neighbors' yards. It was not hard to see who needed to do some yard work, and which fruit trees I could walk by and wish for some fresh fruit to land in front of me. I could even see the cranes on the docks of the port in Liverpool from my vantage point. One of my favorite views, while staring through my window, was watching the birds jumping from one tree to the next, seeing how they would play tag with each other. I also enjoyed watching the clouds float by my bedroom window. Yes, it is evident that I would spend hours staring through my window, contemplating my future.

Remember, I was only eight or nine years old at the time, but it was fun to dream.

I would wonder about my future, and where I would end up. I wondered about what my wife would look like, what type of job I would have, where would I live, would I become a priest, or what would become of me. The questions that raced through my mind were relative to the era in which I grew up. Life intervened, and I grew up. I do believe that I had never lost my ability to think before acting, and I would always consider the consequences of my actions. Childhood dreams start fading, and are stored in a compartment somewhere in your mind. That is, until you reach a stage in your life when you remember those dreams and realize that your eight-year-old self is still very much a part of your life.

Reflections From the Past

My eight-year-old self would never have dreamed that he would be a fifty-something-year-old single dad, living in North Carolina. I highly doubt that he would have had the insight that saw him leaving his Liverpudlian lifestyle at the age of thirty-six to move halfway across the world with his eight-year-old little girl in tow, to start his life all over. I would tell my eight-year-old self to keep doing what he's doing, and not to give up looking for the good in everything. I would also tell him that all his memories, thoughts, and dreams don't disappear just because he is growing up. No one can say when they will return, but they do come back to remind you of where you find yourself. This book is a reminder to my eight-year-old self of how far I have come, and to share some of my observations of what I have picked up over the last forty-something years.

Everything I know as a fifty-something-year-old today is a reflection of my childhood. Dealing with grief has opened that door for me and I know, without a doubt, that Dad is sitting on his heavenly perch and smiling down on us trying to figure things out. Dad is smiling because I am starting to see the lights of realization. Grief doesn't come with a manual. Grief doesn't come with a prescribed template. I have mentioned in my previous books that some of the phrases I have come to hate are: "I know how you're feeling" or "I know what you're going through." I'm not going to tell you that I know how you are feeling when you have had a miscarriage or lost your infant to sudden infant death syndrome (SIDS). I won't tell you that I know what it feels like to lose someone to violence, illness, an accident, or any other means—because I don't know. All I can tell you is that I know what loss feels like. The grief we feel is real, and it can affect all areas of our lives. Helping others has always been a huge part of who I am, and I want to share my experiences with you. This is one of those *sharing-is-caring scenarios* that you can use or ignore. All I want is for everyone to find some peace in a non-judgmental setting.

My eight-year-old self is coming through strongly, with reminders of where we came from and what we felt. The door to the youngster's windowsill-sitting days has been kicked wide open, and I'm loving the reminders, because I am at a place in my life where I know that I am living my best life. I come from a very traditional upbringing where Mum and Dad worked hard to provide us with whatever we needed. We weren't spoiled, but we had enough to make us happy. Did I grow up in a loving family household? Absolutely, without a shadow of a doubt, I did. I was raised in the Catholic faith, which is why I wanted to be a priest, but we all know how that turned out. I know that religion is something not everyone can, or wants to, agree on. I am not going to condemn or judge you based on what you believe. I believe that everyone has a right to their own beliefs.

I am very open with my views on how I see, feel, and interpret things that happen in life. My book—*Life After This: 9 Chapters: History Shows We Have Contacted the Deceased and You Can Do It,*

Too—is a perfect example of my open-minded views. Some may not agree with my views or my assumptions, and many have expressed shock and horror that I would "promote" the views that I do. I am amazed by the reactions because, believe me, I have witnessed "religious" people doing things that are not very Christian-like. All Bible verses I will be sharing from this point onward will be taken from the New International Version. A verse that I would like to share with you comes from Matthew 7:5: "You hypocrite, first take the plank out of your own eye, and then you will see clearly to remove the speck from your brother's eye." This verse is a stark reminder that we should not go about passing judgment on others. I know where I am in my faith, and it may have taken a little bit longer to reach the apex of my spiritual journey, but here I am.

I have an awesome support system of wonderful people, sitting on the opposite side of the condemnation fence, who listen to my views. They may take a little longer to connect the pieces of the puzzle, but they will always come back and thank me for my insight because I have dared to think outside of the box. I don't want to change the way people think. I just want everyone to take a step outside of their bubbles and see things from a different perspective. I promise that you will not be struck down by a lightning bolt for daring to think differently than what you have been taught. Many of my family, friends, acquaintances, and strangers have told me that I have helped them by giving them a glimpse into what a peaceful and calming world would look like by thinking a little differently.

Nature Through My Eyes

I love being outdoors. I haven't gone camping in over 20 years because life always intervened. Then again, you don't have to go camping to enjoy or love nature. One of my favorite pastimes is sitting in my backyard, which overlooks a lake. I can see the ripples in the water, the ducks bobbing up and down while looking for food, and the sound of silence as I retreat into my own little world. Another of my favorite nature activities is hiking in the mountains, finding a secluded spot under the umbrella of trees, and listening to their chatter as the wind tickles their leaves. I can spend hours watching the wildlife frolicking in their natural habitat.

I have found that the distance between me and God is considerably less when I am out in nature. It doesn't matter whether I'm sitting in my backyard, under the umbrella of trees in the forest, hiking in the mountains, or watching a lightning display from my window—God has a hand in all of the different phenomena that are associated with nature. I know that when I have had a hard day, I just have to take a walk around my garden and feel the wind on my skin to know that everything will be okay. I believe that God helps to shape our lives in the way we go about our day, the way we interact with others, and how nothing goes according to our plans. I also believe that God guides us through this maze we call life. He drops many cookie crumbs for us to follow, but more often than not, we choose to ignore those crumbs. I would like this book to be a subtle reminder to keep your eyes out for those cookie crumbs.

The Vision Behind Nature's Reach

The cookie has been broken, and the crumbs are being dropped. All you have to do is to choose the direction in which you want to go. You may currently be hiding between the layers of the cloak of grief, or you may be hovering at the entrance because you are afraid to leave the place where you feel safe. My vision for *Nature's Reach*, pretty much like my other books, is to help people cope with grief. I have interviewed and spoken with many people who have experienced various levels of grief in their lifetimes. I explored many different avenues to help me cope with my grief. There have been times of frustration that I couldn't just "snap out of it" as so many people suggested. Grief doesn't come with a switch that can be turned on or off. Grief doesn't come with a remote control that brings on emotions such as anxiety, anger, or sadness. Grief has an agenda that no one will ever understand because it affects everyone differently.

There is no right or wrong way to cope with grief. No one can tell you how you should be feeling, or what you should be doing to overcome those feelings. Everyone believes that they are an expert in the field of grief. Yes, everyone would be correct, but it should be noted that they are an expert in coping with *their* grief. I'm not here to argue about who does it better because, again, there are no right or wrong answers. Let's take a look at some of the more common types of coping strategies people may use to navigate their way through the cloak of grief. The examples I will be sharing are excellent ways to help fill a void that has been left by the passing of a loved one.

- Some may seek professional therapy from a licensed professional.

- Some may take medication prescribed by medical professionals.

- Some may find healing by talking to friends or family.

- Some may find peace and healing by starting a new hobby or rekindling an old one.

- Some may find comfort and healing by joining a gym or exercising in the privacy of their homes.

- Some may go out and add a new member of the four-foot variety to their family.

These examples, and variations thereof, have been tried and tested by billions of people. We know they work for many, but what about those who can't find that silver cloud or see the light from the depths of the cloak of grief? Not everyone wants to speak to a therapist, take medication, or speak about their feelings with friends or family. Not everyone wants to be stuck doing something they never enjoyed before they were covered by the cloak of grief.

The Journey to Nature's Reach

I wanted to put together a book that offers everyone an alternative method for coping with the grief and the loss of loved ones. This method dates back to the creation of this place we call Earth. Genesis 1:1–31 tells the beautiful story about how God created the earth in six days. Every step of the six days shows readers how God gave us the gift of nature. This gift is something we take for granted because we are so wrapped up in our day-to-day lives. We see the beauty that nature offers us, but we don't appreciate it nearly as much as we should. I believe that God created a universe that holds all the secrets and vital pieces of information for us to live a long and healthy life. I also believe that the beauty of His creation hides many answers and clues for many of the illnesses and pain we experience.

I do believe that there is a natural cure for cancer that doesn't involve chemotherapy or radiation. I do believe that there is a natural cure for asthma that does not involve an inhaler. Again, I am not telling anyone to stop taking their prescribed medication. I am looking at ways to find those natural cures, which include spending time in nature and enjoying the gifts that God has given us—you know, those gifts that we would prefer to complain about, such as the rain that causes damage to our homes, the wind that brings sand to every corner of our homes, or the snow that brings cold.

I would like you to go and stand outside for a couple of minutes. It doesn't matter whether you live in a large city, or a one-horse town where the horse died 50 years ago; stand outside and take a deep breath. Next, I would like you to close your eyes and drown out any distracting sounds such as people talking, children screaming, or car alarms going off. Focus on the sounds of nature; listen to the birds chirping, feel the sun kissing your cheeks, and hear the leaves rustling in the wind. Those are just a couple of the senses that nature has given to us. We are so busy trying to get through a day, a week, or a month that we don't stop to appreciate the small gestures that God has gift-wrapped and hand-delivered to every person who walks on this earth.

Open Invitation

This is your personalized invitation to join me on the next installment of the journey to finding ways to cope with the loss and grief of losing loved ones. Together, we are going to look under every stone, inspect the leaves on plants and trees, learn from the insects, and embrace all the elements that nature sends our way. In short, we are going to rediscover the earth as God intended during the creation. You don't have to be religious to join this journey, and no requirements need to be met. All you are going to need is an open mind, respect for what others may be going through, and an understanding that *everyone is different.* We know that what works for me may not work for you. I love going to the beach and feeling the warm sand between my toes, but others may not share that love. The beauty of this journey is that you get to find your niche—your perfect fit.

Are you ready to discover what nature may have in store for you? Let's get this journey started.

Chapter 1:

Understanding the Human

Central Processing Unit—The

Brain

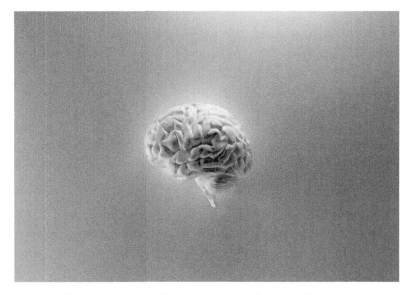

- Have you ever hit your internal pause button to stop and think about what you are doing?

- Have you ever wondered why you were doing something in a specific way?

- Have you ever wondered where your feelings originate from?

The brain or the central processing unit (CPU) plays an important role in our existence. The human body, members of the animal kingdom, household appliances, and motor vehicles rely on their versions of the brain to operate. I have found that we don't think about the whos, whats, and whys when we do something like click a button to turn on the computer or swing the key in the ignition of our vehicles. Many may argue, but I do believe that those are just a hint of many things in our lives that we take for granted. We don't give our brains or the operating systems we utilize much credit. We expect everything to work when we initiate the action, and we are quick to react when something doesn't work.

The brain is responsible for keeping everything running like a well-oiled machine. The heart, lungs, network of veins, and all organs are important to our existence. However, without the brain, those organs will fail to do what they are meant to. The brain is the mastermind behind our actions, reactions, moods, emotions, and feelings. Who or what is going to tell the heart how it must work, or the lungs what they should be doing? I wanted to start off this book by exploring the basics and getting us on the same page. For that to happen, we need to understand the ways of the brain. You don't have to be a brain surgeon to know what is going on inside of your human CPU. I can assure and reassure you that there will be no quizzes, nor will there be any invasive techniques that will test your knowledge and understanding of how the brain operates.

The Model Brain

I have found, especially in the last couple of years, that board-certified medical professionals have had to work harder than normal because of all the newly self-appointed *sofa doctors* who are, and have been, graduating from the Google University of Medicine. The self-appointed sofa doctors have earned themselves degrees in various career paths which include psychiatry, organ retrieval, and surgery. I believe that it is time to redirect our attention and focus to those who have spent many years in their fields of expertise. Doctors, scientists, and researchers at Johns Hopkins Medicine, as with any other medical facility, make it their mission to provide non-medical professionals with information that is relevant to our existence.

Johns Hopkins Medicine presents us with a biology lesson that helps us understand everything we need to know in layman's terms. Did you know that the average adult's brain weighs approximately three pounds? Did you know that our brains consist of approximately 60% fat? Did you know that the 40% of our brain that is not considered to be obese is made up of a combination of salts, carbohydrates, water, and protein? (John Hopkins Medicine, 2021). I may not be a doctor, but I do believe that the sofa medical professionals may just want to put our brains on a low- to no-fat diet after reading some of this information. I have heard people arguing that the brain is a muscle. The composition of the brain, as mentioned, proves that the brain is a solid mass. The brain also features blood vessels, nerves, neurons, and cells that make it the most important part of our bodies. In short, the brain is what keeps us alive without needing mechanical assistance.

Analyzing the Brain

I never paid much attention to the origin of my thoughts, feelings, or emotions until the day I received the call from Dad to tell me that he had been diagnosed with cancer. I will always remember that feeling of shock and disbelief. We don't like to think about the day our loved ones will leave this earth. I know that our time on this earth is not guaranteed. I also know that we live on borrowed time, because we never know when we will be called home. I have spoken to many people over the last two years who have been transparent about their experiences, particularly with them trying to understand their feelings and emotions. One person told me that they would be laughing one moment, and without realizing it, they would be sobbing uncontrollably the next. Another said that they would be "fine" one moment, and then suddenly they would be filled with rage.

This is where I stop and ask again: Where do these feelings and emotions come from, and why do they sneak up on us without prior notice? The brain has a very difficult and complex job, in that it controls everything that makes up our existence. Did you know that the brain doesn't have an on or off button, and it doesn't get to take a break? I have often had people tell me that I should just "turn off my brain" so that I can get some sleep at night. I've tried, and it doesn't work. Realistically, if we have to turn off our brains, we would cease to see another day. However, we can learn how to treat our brain with the respect it deserves by taking care of ourselves. Until that can happen, we need to have an understanding of what the brain has to do.

Discovering How the Brain Works

The brain is the control panel that helps us navigate our daily lives. This is one of those jaw-dropping moments when you realize that *you* aren't the one who gets you out of bed in the morning, helps you see the sun on the horizon, or allows you to have all the different emotions. The control panel in your mind controls the way you think, what you remember, triggers your emotions, and dictates everything you are seeing and feeling, down to your body temperature. The brain is connected to the spinal cord, and together the dynamic duo creates a circuit board that makes up the central nervous system. Ever wondered why you are told to wear a helmet when cycling, riding your scooter, or rollerblading down the road? Yes; to protect your control panel and circuit boards.

The control panel is activated when chemical and electrical currents are transmitted throughout the body. Each part of your body—which includes limbs, muscles, and organs—releases different signals that are processed by the brain. The processes are directed through the appropriate channels that allow you to feel and experience a variety of sensations. The brain features many different chambers, channels, and structures which all play a vital role in our health and well-being. The researchers have pointed out that the brain features three main parts, which are the cerebrum, the brainstem, and the cerebellum. The cerebrum is the front part of the brain, and is home to the cerebral cortex. The cerebral cortex contains two hemispheres which signify the left and right sides of the brain.

The control panel consists of many microchips which are connected by an intricate web of sensors, of which the amygdala is one. The amygdala is located below each of the hemispheres in the cerebrum. The role of the amygdala is to control or regulate each individual's response to their emotions, feelings, and memories. The amygdala is one of the many different types of sensors that can be found buried in the brain, and each one brings something different to the party.

Understanding Why I Feel the Way I Do

I have previously mentioned that we don't always understand why we are laughing and happy one moment, and the next we are sobbing or feeling guilty. I introduced you to the amygdala, which has a permanent home in your brain. The amygdala joins many other sensors that contribute to how the brain reacts without thinking about the actions. I believe that it is safe to assume that most people have activated the autopilot function in their brain so that they don't have to think about what they do, or how they feel. Let's take a look at a couple of the autopilot reactions that you may be doing without thinking:

- Your hair falls in front of your eyes; you brush it away.

- Your nose is running; you reach for a Kleenex to give it a good blow.

- You have an itchy spot on your body; you scratch it.

- You hit your little toe on the corner of your bed; you say "ouch."

- Someone gives you a bunch of flowers; you bring them to your nose to smell them.

These are a couple of examples that I thought would resonate with everyone. I do believe that it would be safe to assume that you are thinking about everything you have been doing. I am fascinated by the autopilot scenario, because it forces us to slow down. We are constantly trying to do everything, and the digital mania we are faced with is not helping us. I believe that we have forgotten how to think about what we are doing. It is important to understand that every part of the brain contributes to our daily lives.

The Effects of Grief

I introduced you to the cloak of grief in *Keep Calm and Cope With Grief: 9 Chapters for Managing Fear and Grief When Losing a Parent or Loved One*. The cloak takes on all shapes and sizes, and allows you to get lost among its layers. Many find solace between the layers, and receive the healing they need to face the world. Others are too afraid to leave, for fear of forgetting the reason for their grief or trauma. Taking a step outside of the cloak of grief reopens wounds because they haven't been properly cleansed and treated. It is part of our natural response to want to do everything for ourselves, and that includes holding onto memories and remembering our loved ones who have passed on. I know that I was reluctant to accept help from those closest to me. I am pretty sure that they would say that I pushed them away. I felt that I needed to be the *knight in shining armor* and be strong for Mum and Gillian. Did I develop a "heroes" complex? Most likely. That has not been a positive experience, because I am in that stage where thoughts and memories come flooding back when I least expect them.

That is when I realized that I was struggling to leave the layers of the cloak of grief. Oh, I could navigate them pretty well, and I still do; but, at least now, I know what is waiting for me on the other side of those layers. It was, and does, protect me from feeling different emotions which include sadness, the desire to pick up the phone to call Dad, anger, and all the questions I never got to ask. You know that grief is separated into two different categories: physical and emotional. The physical effects of grief are visible to those around us which include, and are not limited to:

- insomnia

- sleeping all day

- headaches

- feeling lethargic

- mind fog

- excessive weight loss or gain

- self-care takes a backseat

You may have dealt with grief in a way that satisfies the physical effects. I have determined, after speaking to many of my interviewees, that the majority found themselves dealing with their grief in a way that benefitted them physically. They clawed their way back to reality for many different reasons, such as taking care of their children, needing to work, or keeping busy. Once again, I have to remind you that there is no right or wrong way to cope with loss. One of the biggest pieces of advice my interviewees had to share was that people who experienced a loss need to be kept busy. Some of the ladies started crocheting, knitting, and quilting; others did volunteer work in their communities to help those in need. The takeaway here is that you should keep busy, but always remember to take care of yourself. And a huge piece of advice from me is that it is okay to feel sad, lonely, and angry today. Don't worry about tomorrow because you don't know what tomorrow will bring.

A Message From Your Grief-Stricken Brain

The loss of a loved one comes as a shock, regardless of whether you were prepared or not. A little piece of you hopes that the doctors were wrong. You see all the good days and ignore all the bad ones, because your brain doesn't want to acknowledge that the end is near. I have heard many people say that the family of cancer patients are lucky because they have time to say their farewells. I can tell you that saying farewell, or preparing for the end, is the furthest from your mind when you walk into the room and see your loved one lying in their bed. All you want to do is cram as many good memories into the visit as you can. Someone told me that you should treat each day as if it is the last one, because no one can predict what tomorrow has in store. They also said that you shouldn't spend your precious time thinking about what you didn't do right, and rather focus on making memories that will live on in your mind.

I found an article on the American Brain Foundation's website which was based on a webinar that featured a neurologist, Dr. Lisa Shulman. I found the article enlightening because it tells us how the brain responds to the grief we experience. Doctor Shulman points out that grief wears many hats, which includes the loss of a loved one, medical conditions, abuse, or divorce. The brain picks up on the shift in your mood and starts building an army to protect you. The trigger in your brain will activate the alarm as all the sensors start jumping to attention. Imagine a scenario where you have been informed that someone has suddenly passed away or someone has shared some bad news with you. Your first reaction is shock, your heart drops into your little toe, and you cannot think straight. Your heart starts thumping its way back to your chest as you experience all kinds of emotions, which range between anger and sadness.

Doctor Shulman explains that the brain's reaction to the shock will affect your physical health by increasing your blood pressure and your heart rate. The brain will also send an alert to all the sensors, which will begin the process of releasing hormones that will affect the way you cope with the stress you are feeling. The way you respond to the loss of a loved one, or the grief you are experiencing, affects different people in different ways. Many may not experience grief to the extent that others do, and it doesn't mean that one has more feelings than the other. Some people are better at hiding their grief and don't wear their hearts on their sleeves. Grief doesn't discriminate against anyone, and it doesn't care what age you are, what your gender is, what ethnicity you are, or what your bank balance has to say. This is not a competition, because everyone is affected by grief in some way, shape, or form. Doctor Shulman notes that grief is a natural process that everyone has to go through and experience. Even the toughest person will experience the effects of grief—which they will deny—but you can't fool the brain. Until you are ready to face and cope with your grief, you may find yourself struggling with your memory, your actions and reactions when faced with everyday challenges, a shift in your sleeping pattern, or your physical health.

Repairing the Brain After the Loss of a Loved One

I stumbled across another website that refers to the brain fog you experience when you are grieving. The term that they use is "grief brain," which is a very fitting name for the topic we are learning about. The article reiterates everything that has been discussed in this chapter. Subtle reminders are in place to let grieving warriors know that grief doesn't have an expiration date. I do believe that it is important to know and understand that the grief you are experiencing isn't meant to define you. You are not a weakling for grieving, and you are not a hero for hiding your grief. There is no shame, whatsoever, for feeling the way you do. The second-most important part of this journey is to identify the way your brain acknowledges, understands, and copes with the grief it is experiencing. The first, and most important, part of this journey is to give you alternative methods to help you heal or minimize the effects of grief.

I'm not a therapist, nor am I a medical professional. I am just a regular guy who spends a fair amount of his day overlooking the Outer Banks from his backyard in North Carolina, and soaks up as much of the beauty that nature has to offer. I can't tell you how you should be feeling, nor would I want to, because I don't know what has brought you here. I would like to share a couple of helpful ways to ease the "grief brain" you may or may not be experiencing. Remember that this book is for everyone, and it doesn't matter whether they are struggling to come to terms with the loss of their loved one, put up a wall protecting them from feeling pain and emotions, or dealing with many years' worth of grief. The best gift anyone can give to themselves is that of kindness. Be kind to yourself, treat yourself with the respect you believe you deserve, and take all the time you need to find your way back to your starting point.

Journaling

I believe that journaling is one of the most effective methods to cope with, and heal from, the effects of grief. I have mentioned journaling in my previous books, and it is something that many people utilize for many different reasons. I love that journaling allows me to release all the pent-up feelings in my mind. There is a magical healing power that allows you to be fluid with the paper in front of you. I have had many people tell me that they can't write to save their lives, and they wouldn't know where to start. If I may be so bold as to tell you that anyone can write, and you don't have to think about how or where to start. You don't even have to write in full sentences. Write whatever is in your mind; whether it is negative or positive thoughts. Get those thoughts out of your mind to make room for the healing that will follow.

Patience

Remember that you are not in a race to cope and heal from your grief. Give yourself time to experience all the emotions, and work through them on your own terms. My reminder to you is that anyone who tells you to "snap out of it" doesn't have an ounce of compassion in their body, and the possibility is probable that they have not experienced grief. One of my interviewees told me about an experience they had earlier in the year which opened their eyes to the cold-heartedness of people. My interviewee was hiding between the layers of the cloak of grief because it was the first anniversary of the death of a close relative. The first year is the worst, because the realization sinks in that they will never be returning, and you find yourself with a flood of memories. A friend stopped by and saw that this person had been crying. The friend then told them that they need to stop holding onto the past, and that being sad will not help them. While this may be true, the delivery came across as heartless, with a hint of bullying. The friend never received the memo that they should show support instead of condemnation. Don't ever be afraid to tell others that you deserve respect, and that you require patience while you deal with your grief.

Other Examples

You don't ever have to do anything you do not want to or feel uncomfortable with. We have previously established that what works for me or the next person may not work for you. You have a wealth of resources at your disposal. Did you know that you can take anything and create a coping strategy that will suit you? You could create a digital journal, where you talk into a voice recorder, instead of writing. You could film yourself sharing your feelings. You may decide to share your recordings or videos in the future with people who are struggling. You have the freedom to be as creative as your brain allows you to be. Remember that you are not bound by a contract to the people around you. This is a journey that only *you* get to go through to find *your* healing. Take a look at the list below, and tweak them to work for *you*:

- Lean on others for support.

- Be kind to yourself.

- Perform a cleansing ritual by eliminating negativity.

- Participate in mindful activities such as meditating, yoga, and positive affirmations.

- Lean into your spirituality and faith.

Utilizing One of God's Greatest Gifts

I do believe that God has blessed us with many gifts during our lifetime. I would say that the biggest gift is life. Many may not agree with my assumption because they might feel as if they have been cheated. We have to remember that every person on this earth possesses a soul. The body that was given to our souls is on loan to us. We are placed on this earth for a reason. I know, and understand, that people get angry with God for allowing loved ones to pass away because of illness or violence. Our souls return to heaven the day we die. We are reunited with God and join the other souls as we live on in the hearts and memories of those who love us. We may be angry at God for reclaiming the souls of our loved ones. We may wander off in another direction, away from God, because we are unhappy that parts of our hearts are ripped out. You may be angry right now, and contemplating closing your book or turning off your earpiece.

May I ask, before you close your book or turn off your earpiece, to reconsider your feelings? Do you remember what I asked you in the Introduction? I asked you to keep an open mind. I'm not going to force you to change your views, and there will be no attempt at mind control. I just want the opportunity to show you how seeing religion, faith, and spirituality through the eyes of someone else may be helpful to your journey through the layers of your cloak of grief.

- Do you stop to listen to the choir of chirping birds in your garden?

- Do you stop to admire the hard work and effort that went into the web your resident garden spider has constructed?

- Do you stare out of your window on a stormy day and watch the ducks frolicking in the water?

- Do you run outside when the first snows of the season fall and catch the snowflakes with your tongue?

- Have you ever found a quiet spot on the banks of a river and watched the birds play with the fish?

I believe that one of the greatest gifts, other than life, that God has given us is the gift of nature. We don't give the birds, the mountains, the weather, or the sound of silence the respect it deserves. We are always rushing so much from one point to the other that we take everything in between for granted. I know that many people who are in the grips of grief prefer to be busy, but maybe it is time to slow down and use the gift of nature to help you heal. I have spoken to many people who have said that they prefer working, but that when they have downtime and time to think, they fall apart. Let's see how we can rectify the situation by taking a closer look at the gifts that your Maker has for you.

Chapter 2:

Exploring the Healing Power

Within the Animal Kingdom

The very first book of the Bible takes us on an introductory journey so that we may see and understand how God created the earth. We get to see His vision and intentions materialize in the way that every detail is described. The fifth and sixth days of the creation show me that God had a plan, and that nothing was rushed. Everything was executed as it was meant to be. Genesis 1:20–22 takes us through the fifth day of the creation, and how God populated the water and the sky:

> And God said, "Let the water teem with living creatures, and let birds fly above the etch across the vault of the sky." So God created the great creatures of the sea and every living thing with which the water teems and that moves about in it, according to their kinds, and every winged bird according to its kind. And God saw that it was good. God blessed them and said, "Be fruitful and increase in number and fill the water in the seas, and let the birds increase on the earth."

I like to think that God decided to go big on the sixth day of creation. There were two additions on this day that would complete the vision He had for the perfect earth. Genesis 1:24–25 shows us how His vision would come together:

> And God said, "Let the land produce living creatures according to their kinds: the livestock, the creatures that move along the ground, and the wild animals, each according to its kind." And it was so. God made the wild animals according to their kinds, the livestock according to their kinds, and all the creatures that move along the ground according to their kinds. And God saw that it was good.

The second addition to the sixth day is the introduction of man, along with God's instructions on how to care for the animal kingdom that He created in Genesis 1:26:

Then God said, "Let us make mankind in our image, in our likeness, so that they may rule over the fish in the sea and the birds in the sky, over the livestock and all the wild animals, and over all the creatures that move along the ground."

I do believe that it is safe to say that God gave us a massive gift when he created the animal kingdom. I know that many people will argue or disagree with the Word as quoted, because so much has changed since God created the earth. Besides, if you have been around, you will know that I am very open-minded. I believe that we have to adapt to the new world we find ourselves in. It doesn't matter whether the millions of different species have been crossbred, have lost their original names, or have been reallocated to different hierarchies within the animal kingdom; the fact remains that they are still God's creation.

This chapter is not about challenging the Bible, your dietary habits, your religion, or your faith, nor is it about animal activists jumping on their moral bandwagon. The animal kingdom plays a very important role in our existence. It is thanks to the members of the animal kingdom that we are alive and thriving today. The animal kingdom contributes a lot more to the world than we give them credit for, which is why I have chosen to include them in *Nature's Reach*.

The Animal Kingdom Offers More Than Feel-Good and Cuddly Animals

- Do you spontaneously break into a smile when you see animals?

- Do you feel all warm and fuzzy on the inside when you are watching videos featuring animals?

- Do you think that members of the animal kingdom make the world a better place?

If you have answered "yes" to one or all of the questions, then you are part of a society that believes that the animal kingdom is important to our existence. I dug around the trenches, visited various websites, and spoke to many people to find out what the animal kingdom is comprised of. My research led me in a couple of different directions, where I was left laughing because I know that many people would not agree with my findings. I would like to insert it here; that I believe with every fiber of my being, that God has a sense of humor when it comes to certain members of His animal kingdom. I only have to mention certain insects, critters, rodents, or reptiles to invoke different types of reactions. I have witnessed people running away screaming when they see spiders and rodents. Others nearly pass out on the spot when they see certain reptiles from the slithering family. The knee-jerk reaction—when spotting these darling members of the animal kingdom—is to squish, squash, or spray them to death.

Every member of the animal kingdom serves a purpose—even when we refuse to acknowledge or see it. The animal kingdom is made up of mammals, reptiles, amphibians, birds, fish, and everything in between. It is important to remember that every one of the creatures in the animal kingdom contributes to how we live. It doesn't matter whether they are domesticated or wild; they all play an important role in nature and add value to human life. Please join me for a quick walkthrough, as I show you a couple of examples of what members of the animal kingdom contribute.

Value Added Animals that Bring Healing and Reparation to the Environment

I recently saw a photo of a young lady holding four baby rats in the palm of her hand. The comment section of this photo had me laughing out loud. However, it made me think that this would be the perfect example of members of the animal kingdom that are helpful to the environment. Many people would be fawning over these baby rats, but others would form picket lines to have them permanently removed from society. I understand why some people may feel the way they do, because rodents do present a problem when being left to fend for themselves. One may say that they attend the *School of Life: Outcasts United.* We all know the destruction that certain members of the animal kingdom are capable of. I do believe it is safe to say that most of us have been at the other end of the mouse droppings, chewed boxes and plastic packages, or gnawed-at electrical wires.

The United States Department of Agriculture's Natural Resources Conservation Service tells us that ALL animals play an important role in the ecosystem. The ecosystem relies on wild animals which include fish, insects, rodents, and birds to keep the environment in perfect harmony (NRCS, 2020). It is important to respect the process that the ecosystem goes through. Let's take a closer look at the importance of having undesirable members of the animal kingdom in our environment, and how they keep the balance of the ecosystem.

Rats

- What is the purpose of rats?

- What would happen if rats became extinct?

Love them or hate them, rats are important to the ecosystem. Yes, they may be pests. Yes, they may be destructive. Yes, they are scavengers. The reality is that they are fighting for survival. I know that many rats have crept their way into the hearts of animal lovers. Many have shared that they rescued rat pups from becoming reptile dinners, and others have proudly shared how they had domesticated their rescues. I'm not here to tell you to release them into the wild, nor am I going to tell you to remove them from existence. I am here to share the way nature works, and what its purpose is to the ecosystem.

Rats eat whatever we discard, whether it is scraps of food, garden refuse, or whatever you are removing from your home. The rats, when plumped up and out hunting for food, will attract the attention of predators such as falcons, owls, hawks, and whoever is out hunting. Rats are also a vital element in the dietary needs of reptiles and amphibians. We risk destroying the ecosystem if we were to eradicate all the rats from the environment. I also found out that rats are used to detect landmines in war-stricken territories. It is said that rats have sensitive noses and can sniff out landmines. It is believed that they are more effective than metal detectors. I believe that rats may be more efficient in the height and weight departments because they won't trigger the plates as they flit around the areas. I am not saying that we should rescue all rats, and I am not saying that we should go on a killing spree; I am saying that we should respect the environment and trust the ecosystem to do what it is meant to do according to the creation.

Insects

Insects, like rats, are public enemies in the eyes of humans. My research into the topic of how nature can help us with the loss of loved ones opened up many doors. You may be thinking that you have gone from being a brain surgeon to a biologist, conservationist, and animal activist. You are exactly where you need to be because everything that I am sharing with you is going to help you understand how nature works, and how nature can help you cope with your feelings.

Insects are not on everyone's pro list. We are quick to complain about them being a nuisance and a menace. A natural reaction is to swat or spray them with insecticide. Would you change your mind if I told you that approximately one-third of the food that is grown is dependent on insects? We wouldn't be alive and reading this book if it weren't for the pollinator insects. Pollination is essential for crops to grow, flowers to bloom, and trees to produce oxygen. Human lives would be in a lot of trouble if bees, butterflies, wasps, or ants were removed from the environment. We wouldn't have viable crops to feed the wildlife, domesticated animals, and humans if we eradicated all the insects. The ecosystem will collapse.

Birds

I have opted to place our feathered friends in this section because they are just as important to the environment as they are to our family lives. Birds, like insects, play a vital role in keeping the balance of the ecosystem. They assist with pollinating crops, plants, and trees. I previously mentioned that predators of the winged variety feast on rodents, which is nature's way of controlling pests and overpopulation.

Our feathered friends—which include turkeys, geese, ducks, penguins, robins, hummingbirds, and chickens—have become family members to many people. I know that not everyone will agree with me, but I know of many homesteads across the country, and the world, that have these birds roaming around their properties. Not everyone wants to make a Thanksgiving, Christmas, or Easter meal out of them. Homesteaders raise these birds to help their farms, which is an extension of the ecosystem. They eat grains that go through the channels (digestive system), and join the land as fertilizer. They also eat vegetable and fruit scraps that would otherwise rot and attract unwanted pests, which are also consumed.

Finding Healing and Therapy Within the Animal Kingdom

I will plead the fifth if your spouse, partner, or parents were to email me with messages admonishing me for recommending that you purchase or adopt one, two, or many new family members. No one should be buying or adopting pets based on someone else's experiences or suggestions. Just because your uncle adopted a golden retriever doesn't mean that you should adopt one. Adding a member of the animal kingdom to your family involves many deciding factors and considerations. I am going to list a couple of questions that I want you to think about:

- Why do you want a pet?

- Do you have time to be a pet owner?

- Can you afford to take care of your pet's grooming, medical care, and food?

- Do you have a backup plan if you have to leave town for work or go on vacation?

You will need to be brutally honest when answering the questions. Animals, regardless of breed or species, have feelings. They come from various backgrounds, which may not have been shared with you. You may come across as the hero when you proudly announce the adoption of Lenny the tortoise, or Jackson the bunny. You may never know that Lenny was removed from his natural habitat in the mountain and kept in an enclosure in someone's backyard for more years than anyone would know. Jackson may have been kept in a crate most of his life, and has never felt grass under his little paws. We don't know what goes on in their little minds. All they know is what they have experienced, and they won't know the difference between right and wrong. These two scenarios apply to all members of the animal kingdom.

I know that grief affects people in different ways, but have you ever thought about the grieving process of an animal? Allow me to tell you the story about Ella, the miniature Maltese poodle. Ella was purchased at the age of six weeks. Ella was a spoiled little princess who could do no wrong. Ella's original owner moved to a different state, and left her with her mother. She would follow her all over the house, and when it was time for bed, Ella could be found beside her. Sadly, Ella's new owner passed away suddenly, and she was left dazed and confused. Ella wasn't all alone because she had her "sister" now. Little Ella sat at the window for six weeks after the original owner's mother passed away, waiting for her to return. Poor little Ella had been abandoned by her original owner, and watched her new owner leave this earth—all this happened within the space of the first four years of her life. This story ends well, and Ella is living out the best years of her life with her "sister" and four-legged sister. She is still the princess, she sleeps right next to her "sister," and she perks up when she hears mention of her previous two owners.

Ella's story may have turned out well because she stayed in the family, but one can only imagine what she was thinking. When I had heard that she sat at the window waiting for her recently departed mother to return home, I had a lump in my throat. I was told that Ella would cry whenever her new mother went to the store, and the neighbor would call and tell her to get home because her dog was crying. Whoever believes that animals have no feelings needs to spend some time at one of the many rescue facilities in their county.

Understanding Senses and Feelings

Did you know that animals and humans share the same senses? Animals have an advantage when it comes to utilizing their senses, because they are more fine-tuned than humans. These are some of the gifts I referred to in Chapter 1, that we take for granted. Our senses are tied to our existence, and without them, we become angry and frustrated. We have the ability to express how we are feeling when something doesn't go the way we want it to.

I do believe that we can learn a lot from animals. They are like sponges who soak up everything that they are dealt with. They are unable to talk back, and they can't tell us what they need. They rely on us to interpret what they need, and in some instances, they will show you their needs. Animals require the same amount of unconditional love and respect that they bestow on us. Do I include members of the wildlife variety under the same umbrella? Why should they be excluded? They are animals. They may have different needs than our domesticated variety, but they are animals with the exact same senses and feelings.

Sight

The gift of vision is something that we, humans and animals, are blessed with. It is also a gift that can be taken away without much notice. You don't know how reliant you are on your sight until you don't have it, or when you start squinting to read the fine print on your paperwork. We are lucky, in the sense that we have coping strategies in place to help us navigate our blindness. Unfortunately, animals are not that lucky. They rely on their vision to help protect them and to keep them well fed. Without their eagle-eyed vision, they are not going to survive in the world. An animal without vision will feel lost, alone, and afraid.

Hearing

We rely on our hearing to help us identify the different sounds that we may or may not take for granted. I have previously asked if you stop and take a moment during your busy day to listen to the birds twittering or the leaves rustling in the breeze. Block your ears for a couple of minutes and imagine not hearing anything but your heart beating. An animal without its hearing is not as devastating as a blind animal, but it is a hindrance because they rely on their hearing to identify potential danger. An animal's hearing is more defined than humans, and they can hear sounds in the distance. They will send out a national alert by the animal council to let everyone know that there is a shift in the weather, or that danger is imminent. Can you imagine being a dog with no hearing, and your owner is telling your siblings that it is time to go and explore the neighborhood?

Smell

I believe that we are born smellers or sniffers. Okay, so we may not be walking around the stores with our noses on other shoppers' butts, but we do go around sniffing and smelling everything we see. I believe that we do take the gift of smell for granted, because we accept that roses will have a certain aroma or that your cinnamon rolls will smell delicious. Animals use their sense of smell to determine friends from foes, or know when they are entering an area that has been marked by another animal. I think that it would be safe to assume that animals and humans are on the same page when it comes to the sense of smell and the feelings it comes with.

- **protection from possible danger:** Animals may be alerted to an enemy, and humans may be alerted to fire or a gas leak.

- **appetite:** Animals and humans use their sense of smell to let them know that they are hungry.

- **emotions:** Smelling a certain aftershave or perfume will open some memories that have been in hiding.

Taste

Humans and animals share the same love for the sense of taste because they involve food. The human taste buds may be a little more refined than those of animals, but it is safe to assume that everyone is on a very similar page. I spoke to someone who told me that their partner had a rule for the children. Instead of pulling their noses up to the food they were given, they were introduced to one new item of food each week. The rule was that they had to take a bite of the new item every day without complaining. If that item was brussels sprouts—it would be a bite every day, and if they didn't like it after seven days, they would never have to eat it again. I know of someone else who tried the same method with their dogs, and introduced animal-friendly fruit and vegetables into their diet. Where the dogs were treated with cookies and the occasional pieces of non-chocolate candy, they decided to introduce carrots, apples, mango, and watermelon—to name a few. It took some time for the dogs to learn to enjoy the fruit and vegetables, but now they take a piece of candy or cookie, play with it, and leave it without eating it. Instead, they know where the fruit and vegetables are kept, and will sit in front of the refrigerator until they get their "something" from the drawers.

Touch

This is one of the senses I believe everyone needs to treasure. The sense of touching and feeling is built around our emotions. I am a firm believer in sharing the gift of touch with those around us, without infringing on anyone's personal space. This is one of those moments when you will pick up on others' boundaries, and if you want someone (or animals) to trust you; show your respect by respecting them.

The Trust Between Man and Members of the Animal Kingdom

Is it possible to build a trusting relationship between yourself and members of the animal kingdom? I love to believe that it is not only possible, but it is doable, as well. We have been conditioned to believe that chickens should be in a coop, rabbits in a hutch, horses in a paddock, or deer in a forest. No one stops to think that these animals may just want a little bit of human interaction. I know that many may frown upon having chickens as pets, or hand-feeding a deer that has decided that she likes your yard. I recall hearing someone telling me that when you are the host of wild animals or birds, it is an indication that you are trustworthy, respectful, and kind. I tend to agree with that assessment. I was also told that any animals that visit your property can sense your feelings. Another scenario that was shared was that, if you are visited by wild animals or birds; it could be your loved one visiting as an animal. I like all the examples that were given to me, because that is the way my mind works. I see the visits and sightings of various members of the animal kingdom as a sign that Dad or Amadeus are visiting.

Once upon a time, I was a human pet dad of two chickens. They would follow me around, and not just because I came with the food bucket, but because they wanted to be with me. I could talk to them, and they wouldn't give me a mouthful. I enjoyed having them around because they made me feel happy, and calmed me down after a long, tedious day at work. Sadly, they died several years ago. I had them cremated at the local pet cemetery, and when they came home, I placed their ashes next to my fireplace.

I realize the important role Amadeus played in my life as I work on this chapter. He was a permanent fixture in my life for 15 years—never far from me. We went through so much together, and he was my little sounding board. I would talk to him the way I would if he were a human being. I would share everything with him; from my highs to my lows, and everything in between. We played, ate, and slept together. I never realized it back then, and it wasn't something that was widely known, but Amadeus was my therapy or support buddy. I didn't know just how soothing it was to stroke, pet, or tickle him. We stayed fit together as he joined me on my runs, and when we went for walks along the lake. I hope that he knows that I was there for him as much as he was there for me.

I miss my little buddy. Reliving those last days of his life is hard. I miss Amadeus as though he only just left this earth to join Dad on his heavenly perch. I'm man enough to admit that I have days where the tears flow. I feel the ache in my heart that I can't describe. I am not ashamed to say that I grieve for my dog. No one should ever be ashamed to grieve. I have found that one of the most helpful forms of healing is sharing your story with others so that they may find something that helps them.

I have a new friend who showed up in my backyard shortly after Amadeus joined Dad. I am pretty sure that he sent her to me. I have named her Samantha, and she is a very fetching young lady deer. Samantha is about five years old, and visits several times a day. She just saunters through the backyard as if she has been doing it for years. She is a very sweet girl, very calm, and an excellent listener—yes, I do talk to her, as well. It has taken approximately three months for this young lady to learn how to trust me. I didn't intrude on her boundaries, and I allowed her to set the pace. Samantha is now a connoisseur who has developed a palate for sweet corn, especially the apple-flavored variety, and enjoys her snacks from the palm of my hand.

We have worked out a schedule that involves me looking into the backyard from the window to see if Miss Samantha is waiting patiently for her breakfast. I walk out with her corn; she meets me halfway, and eats her breakfast from my hand. She allows me to stroke her neck and tickle behind her ears. I look into her eyes, which are trusting and calm, and I believe that I can see her smiling at me. Some days you will find me sitting on the rock wall so that we are face-to-face. I had no idea how beautiful deer are. Many may frown and tell me that it is dangerous, but I trust her and I know she trusts that I won't hurt her. I have talked to Samantha about Dad and Amadeus, and I find myself wondering if she can sense my sadness.

I believe that Samantha was sent to me by God. He knows how much pain I am feeling. God is showing me that His animal kingdom can help people like me, you, and whoever needs a nature "kick" to help us cope with our loss and grief. The similarities between Amadeus and Samantha may be night and day, but they are residents of the animal kingdom and they listen as if they understand our stories, pain, complaints, and heartache. This is where having an open mind comes into play, because if you don't have an open mind, you won't be able to experience the beauty of the world around you.

Chapter 3:

Help! Understanding Why the

Weather Affects My Moods

I would like to introduce you to the four seasons that play an essential role in the weather patterns all across the globe: summer, fall, winter, and spring. Many of us have a love or hate relationship with the four seasons. The topic of weather and the seasons is one we can all agree to disagree on, because everyone has an opinion about which season is the best, worst, and so-so. It's okay if one-quarter of the population agrees with your views. Do you really want to waste your energy on arguing about whether winter is the best season, or that spring brings about health concerns such as allergies? No, you don't. I can assure you that you don't want to argue about something you have no control over. I do believe that you will walk away with a headache, elevated blood pressure, and anger because someone dared to express their views that didn't align with yours. This is where I will implore you to build a bridge, walk over it, and burn the bridge behind you.

This chapter is not about which season is the most popular, most unbearable, or most destructive. I wanted to explore the idea of *how* and *why* the different types of weather affect our moods, emotions, and feelings. This book is, after all, about discovering ways in which nature can help us cope with the loss of our loved ones.

- Do you believe that the weather plays a role in your mobility?

- Do you feel as if you are in a slump when the weather changes?

- Do you find yourself struggling with intense headaches during certain seasons?

I would like you to think about these questions. I have previously mentioned that we don't stop to think about the finer details of our lives. We are so busy trying to do everything that we forget to think about what is happening inside us.

Asking and answering questions is a good way to help you slow down. You are forced to think, and when you do, you are allowing your mind to register your innermost feelings. That is when you realize that you have missed some of the tell-tale signs that you have been blocking your feelings, to protect yourself from the pain and grief you are experiencing. Remember that this chapter is not about your love or hate relationship with summer, fall, winter, or spring; it is about the weather conditions and how they may, or may not, affect you.

My Mental and Emotional Well-Being Versus the Weather Conditions

Scientists and researchers believe that climate change is one of the largest contributors to the state of our mental and emotional health and well-being. They note that people may spiral out of control if they were faced with, or believe that, extreme weather conditions are threatening their lives. These conditions include—and are not limited to—hurricanes, tornados, flash floods, drought, or blizzards. The fear of these events happening may induce stress, which in turn could have adverse effects that lead people to self-harm, consume alcohol, or indulge in illegal drug use. Many of these fears and "self-treatment" regimes spread the doors wide open for any number of issues such as suicidal thoughts, attempted suicide, suicide, or overdosing on illegal or prescription drugs (Crimmins et al., 2016).

The cloak of grief is a place of refuge. It is easily accessible during times when you are feeling overwhelmed, missing your loved ones, or when fear of forgetting seeps in. We put on brave faces when we have to go to work or socialize with people. Most of the time we do a pretty good job at masking our feelings; but, in the blink of an eye, *something* happens and we don't make it to the cloak of grief in time. That *something* could come in the form of a gust of wind that turns into a windstorm. It could be a torrential downpour that has you trapped in your home. Maybe it is the hot summer days that have you sweating bullets and panting for cold air. Let me ask you a question that I want you to put in the back of your mind as you continue reading: Do you believe that the weather affects the way you cope with your grief?

Scientists have been asking the same question for years. They have used many different test subjects, weather and mood variables, and countless hours of studying the effects that the weather may or may not have on people. Carolyn Gregoire wrote a very interesting and science-backed article—*The Surprising Ways the Weather Affects Your Health and Well-Being*—for the HuffPost, an online media publication. The article mentions that people living in certain areas may be exposed to various traumas because of the high-risk tendencies for weather conditions such as hurricanes, flash floods, tornadoes, or even tsunamis. Fear inserts itself into every fiber of people's lives, and that does not equate to living a happy, healthy, and calm life. The National Wildlife Federation has predicted that approximately 200 million Americans—allow that number to sink in—will most likely be diagnosed with disorders such as stress, severe anxiety disorder, self-harming, suicide, or turning to the illegal use of narcotics and alcohol (Gregoire, 2017).

- Do you believe that the weather affects the way you cope with your grief?

- Would it be possible to use the weather to your advantage?

- Do you think that you could cancel out the negative experiences by creating positive scenarios?

Blame It on the Weather—Or Not

I enjoy sharing my experiences but, as you may recall, I am not a medical professional. I do a lot of research, and I rope in my publisher and editor to help me find proof of what I am saying. Studies have proven that climate change has an effect on people's moods, and scientists have even given it a name—seasonal affective disorder (SAD). Staff writers for the Mayo Clinic note that SAD is one of the labels pinned on one of the many different types of depression that we may experience. The name suggests that SAD is responsible for our feelings, moods, and emotions based on the seasons and weather variables that follow. Many may not agree with the assessment, while others may be sitting upright, paying attention, and resonating with what is being said.

You may be asking yourself any number of questions right now, to assess whether you suffer from SAD. Remember to consult your medical professional before self-diagnosing any illnesses, disorders, or conditions. This book is not about canceling out the middleman and jumping straight from an assumption to a diagnosis. Please don't mess with your health—be it physical, mental, or emotional. Medical professionals study for many years to get to the stage where they are allowed to diagnose patients or refer them through the correct channels. Professor Google and his many associates may offer their views, but they are just a Band-Aid that can't offer a long-term solution for a long-term medical condition.

SAD Symptoms

What leads you to suspect that you may be suffering from SAD? I'm so happy that you have asked, and I would love to share some of the symptoms that you may experience. Please remember that the symptoms will vary from person-to-person, and situation-to-situation. The list, as shared by the Mayo

Clinic, is not set in stone. Some people may experience one or two of the symptoms, others may experience the whole, and many may not even realize that they are feeling different until they are made aware. They include:

- waking up exhausted

- feeling as if you are being weighed down

- not caring to participate in favorite pastimes such as watching movies, gardening, or baking

- lacking the energy to do simple tasks, such as folding the laundry or unpacking the dishwasher

- sleeping patterns affected; sleeping too much or not sleeping

- giving in to the temptation of consuming snacks that lead to overeating and, ultimately, gaining weight

- a non-existent appetite, possibly leading to extreme weight loss and eating disorders

- losing focus when trying to concentrate on any specific task on hand

- believing that you are not worthy of happiness, and being wracked with guilt for any negative thoughts

- feelings of anxiousness

- taking your frustrations and irritability out on those closest to you

Medical Risks Related to SAD

I know that I keep reminding you to consult a medical professional for a diagnosis. I have to emphasize, as many times as is needed, that your health and well-being are on the line. One of the best gifts that you could give yourself is the practice of self-care. The list of symptoms I have shared may lead to several risk factors if left untreated. You may read over the list and identify one of the symptoms, but dismiss it as being nothing important. You won't know what is relevant and what is not if you don't go for regular checkups. Let's take a look at some of the risk factors that may be associated with SAD (Mayo Clinic Staff, 2021).

- familial history of depression

- mental disorders, such as bipolar

- vitamin D deficiency

I believe that you, me, and everyone else can do anything we put our minds to. With a little change here, and a tweak there, you can mold and sculpt your future to be whatever your heart desires. You don't have to be afraid that you will forget your loved ones. No one can erase the memories you have; they are yours to keep for all of your eternity. Are you ready to continue on this journey to see if we can discover ways to transform the negative, fear-mongering weather conditions into something that will entice us to leave the safety of the cloak of grief? Let's take a look at the weather conditions to see how it can help people like you and me to find that inner peace, calm, and beauty our wounded souls require.

Nature's Therapy: Looking toward the Weather for Healing

I do believe it is safe to assume that the weather plays a larger-than-life part in our daily lives. I can just imagine that you are reading through the list of symptoms, a couple of times, and thinking about your feelings. You may even be armed with your notebook and pen, and making lists to see if the signs and symptoms that I shared are an accurate representation. The minuscule signs of skepticism that you had when you started reading this book are beginning to fade away. Many of your unasked questions are being answered the more you learn about what your mind is going through. The more you read, listen, and understand what is being presented, the clearer your vision becomes. What happens when your mind starts understanding the *whos*, *whats*, *whens*, and *whys*? That is when I know that the healing that I have been craving is not too far behind.

Every day is a gift, because you never know what tomorrow will bring. The sun may be shining brightly, and the skies may be blue today. You may wake up tomorrow morning, and be greeted with an overcast day and clouds threatening to explode. I often find myself wondering how meteorologists predict the weather for a week at a time. Do they have a direct line to heaven? I would love to work with them, because that would mean I could hear Dad's voice each day as we predict what tomorrow will bring. If only it were that easy.

I always look for the good in everything. I may not always like what I'm trying to extract the positive from—thunderstorms or blizzards - but who am I to look a gift horse in the mouth. I have learned to look beyond my comforts and needs, and appreciate everything I am given. I may not enjoy the rain, but I know that it is needed. I may not like the icy cold weather, but it plays an important role in the environment. I may not like spring because it triggers allergies, but I know that it is part of what makes the birds sing and the flowers bloom. I may be angry at having to rake up leaves in the fall, but I know that it needs to happen to enable trees to heal and recover for the season of rebirth. It's okay not to like certain seasons, but we have to be grateful for what they present us with each day. I would like to leave you with some food for thought as you contemplate revising your relationship with the weather. John Ruskin says: "Sunshine is delicious, rain is refreshing, wind braces us up, snow is exhilarating; there is really no such thing as bad weather, only different kinds of good weather" (John Ruskin Quotes, n.d., para. 1).

Don't Go Away Rain

Have you heard the nursery rhyme that tells the rain to go away and come back another day? How about the one where an old man snoring and how he couldn't get up in the morning is mentioned? I think it is safe to say we all know those timeless classics that we grew up singing with enthusiasm, and many of us believed that the weather gods could hear us when the rain would slow down. I'm here to, hopefully, change the way you think about the rain. This is where I will ask you to open your mind, ever so slightly, to visualize what I am conveying.

The rain is not your enemy. Did you know that the word "rain" is not mentioned in the Bible until Genesis 7:4: "Seven days from now I will send rain on the earth for forty days and forty nights, and I will wipe from the face of the earth every living creature I have made." Rain wasn't necessary, especially such a drastic measure, until Adam and Eve sinned by disobeying when tricked into eating the forbidden fruit. Whatever happened, happened—and we can't go back to change the past. You shouldn't allow your feelings toward the rain to dictate how you feel.

- Who are you really angry with?

- Is it the rain you are angry with, or is it that you can't do your daily chores?

- Is the rain preventing you from working in the garden?

- Is someone going to walk through the muddy puddles and dirty your clean floors?

- Are you missing your daily walk or jog?

Change the way you think about something you don't like—it doesn't have to be rain; it could be anything that raises your blood pressure. Spend time in meditation or prayer when it rains. Close your eyes, block out distracting sounds, and focus on the pitter-patter of the rain as it hits your windows. You could sit at the window and journal your feelings as the water spills from the clouds and lands in your garden. I do believe that there is nothing more relaxing than lying in bed, listening to the sounds of the rain as it meets the roof, and falling asleep. Someone once told me that they believed that the rain represents cleansing and growth. They said that God is cleaning the sidewalks, so that new footprints can walk along the path and grow with the world. Remember, the rain is not meant to make your life miserable. You don't have to love it, but you should be grateful because it is a gift that can be taken from you when least expected.

Embracing the Sunlight

Summer is a season that brings attention to the sun and all that it comes with such as heat, profuse sweating, being uncomfortable, sunburn, or skin cancer. You would do well to remember that summer only lasts for a couple of months, so it wouldn't be fair to build your relationship with the sunlight on the backbone of summer. The sun will always be around, unless it is hidden by rain or clouds. Why won't the sun go away when summer has packed its bags? That is a very valid question, and the answer may just surprise you—or not. We need the sun. The sun is an important fixture in our lives. Without it, we wouldn't have natural light, and life as we know it would cease to exist.

Can you honestly say that you don't enjoy being outside, working in the garden, playing football with friends, cycling, or hiking? As I have previously pointed out, we don't think about the benefits until it is pointed out to us. We are all well acquainted with the seasons. Oh yes, we know about the extreme heat and we know how it makes us feel during summer. Did you know that the sun shines during fall, winter, and spring too? Of course you did, but the fall sun is not the same as the summer sun—until you realize that the sun is not a season. Spending time outdoors comes with more positive benefits than negatives. The medical professionals suggest you take the necessary precautions, such as using an effective sunscreen and protecting your eyes to safeguard them from the UVB rays, as well as staying hydrated.

The benefits of spending time in the sunlight include:

- strengthens your immune system

- alleviates pain

- allows you to relax

- sharpens your internal senses

- helps to reduce the effects of depression

- improves your sleeping habits

- exposes you to vitamin D

Spend time outside when you are feeling as if the walls are closing in on you, or when you are missing your dearly departed a little more than normal. Spend time meditating or praying. Focus on the sounds of nature: chirping birds, leaves gently rustling in the breeze, or the water splashing against the rocks of the lake. Feel the sun pixies as they jump around on your skin to avoid burning their little feet. Don't be afraid to step into the sunlight. Find a ray with your name on it, and draw all the energy you need from it. You may find yourself feeling a little "lighter" if you expose your cloak of grief to some sunlight.

Nature's Therapy: Embracing All Weather Conditions—Part 1

I have spoken to many people who have been forthcoming and willing to share their opinions regarding the weather and how it affects them. Many have said that they never knew that SAD was an official diagnosis for something they had been experiencing for years. It is a well-known fact that we can't control the weather, or what happens in our minds, bodies, and souls when it rains, the wind blows, or when the sun is blazing down on us. Our only defense against the weather conditions is to adapt to what is going on and protect ourselves—instincts kick in. The weather is not your enemy, nor are the seasons. There are no hidden agendas or ulterior motives from the weather camp. I am pretty sure that Mother Nature never intended to make your life miserable. God never gives us more than we can handle. Many may not agree with my assessments, and that is perfectly fine. I have learned to adapt to all types of weather conditions because I know that every aspect of the weather is designed for a purpose.

I am not an expert on the weather conditions, and I can't speak for anyone other than myself. I have learned that it doesn't help me or anyone else when I complain about the weather. I started holding myself accountable for my thoughts and ran them through a filter before speaking. I experienced a shift in my mindset somewhere along the lines, and I am now at the point where the weather has a big impact on me—not in a negative way. I love and enjoy the summertime. I find that I have more energy and I am invigorated with a get-up-and-go attitude. Winter, on the other hand, slows me down and makes me think more—this is a good thing. I remember that the rain affected me all through my childhood and into adulthood. I want to be closer to the rain; so, you would most likely find me sitting on the patio or at the window; listening and watching the rain in silence. The pitter-patter, as it falls on the roof or hits the window, has a mesmerizing effect on me. The spirit inside my soul comes alive at the sight and sound of the rain. Why would it affect me like this? Why is it that the sight and sounds awaken my senses in this manner? Why does it feel as if I am being enveloped in a calming embrace by the sight and sounds that the rain brings?

I previously mentioned that, as a child, I would sit on the windowsill of my bedroom for hours. The weather conditions never bothered me as I sat staring out of my window. I had the best view, and I could see near and far. The rain always affected me a little differently. I always seemed to be at peace with whatever was going on in my life. For some reason or another, I was always a little calmer when it rained, and I could concentrate for longer periods when studying for the school exam. I would be filled with peace when contemplating my future which included where I would live, what type of job I would have, who I would marry, and how many children I would have. There is just something special, peaceful, and calming about the rain that lifts the weight off one's shoulders.

I am an outdoorsy type of person. I love being out in nature. I would take Jessica camping quite frequently when I was younger. There is just something magical about sleeping outdoors and inhaling lungs full of fresh air that opens all the doors to your mind, body, and soul. You experience a sense of peace and tranquility. In the event that it should rain on one of these camping excursions, we would lie in the tent and listen to the raindrops dripping down on us. The sound of the rain falling on the tent is enough to put anyone in a trance. I could listen to those sounds for hours, and I would allow my mind to walk through memory lane. I would find myself thinking about Mum and Dad, disagreements, and petty arguments (normal sibling stuff) with Gillian, my job, or my boss. I think about two of my grandmas, who are sitting beside Dad on his heavenly perch. I think about how much I miss them, and that I look forward to the day that we will be reunited.

I would venture out into the rain, armed with my umbrella, when gazing out the window made me long to be outside. I would walk to the local community park, Derby Park, which was not more than 200 yards away from my childhood home. I would stroll around the park, find a dry bench under some trees, and make myself comfortable. I would sit there for hours, my mind thinking about what I wanted to do, and contemplate the future—the normal "boy meets world" type of thoughts. I loved to listen to the rain hitting the leaves of the trees that were shielding me, and wait for the "plop" as it hit the umbrella. I would stare at the drops of rain as they fell on the bushes and created a mini waterfall as they crashed to the ground. I would watch as the rain formed pools of water on the ground—just waiting for a child to come along, wearing their rain boots, and jump in the puddles. There is nothing more healing for the soul than embracing the weather conditions and turning your negatives into positives.

The weather conditions may have a negative effect on people, but you shouldn't allow it to prevent you from experiencing the healing effects it comes with. I hadn't properly grieved for Dad when Amadeus crossed over the rainbow bridge. I have found solace in the weather; especially when it rains. I will go and sit out on the patio, or at the window during a rainstorm. I block out everything around me, and I end up on a planet that no man has claimed. I am alone on that planet, where I can only see and hear the rain. I will watch the raindrops start a marathon on the windowpane in front of me. I watch the droplets grow in size as they race to the finish line. My focus turns to the branches of the trees outside, as the wind and the rain work in tandem to ensure they get in a good workout.

Nature's Therapy: Embracing All Weather Conditions—Part 2

I have spoken in depth about how the rain makes me feel, but I never got around to explaining the effects of the sun. I have mentioned that I love the summertime. Being out in the sun and experiencing nature is as rewarding as embracing cold, wet, and gloomy weather. Summertime, for me, means being outdoors and working in the garden or interacting with my garden guests. I introduced you to Samantha in Chapter 2.

Samantha has a friend, whom I have named Mrs. Brown. Yes, Mrs. Brown is also a deer and, like Samantha, I have started feeding her by hand. I feel like Dr. Doolittle or an animal whisperer who lets the wild animals know that they have a safe place to visit and that they can trust us. Getting these two lovely ladies to trust is not something that can be done during a rainstorm because it takes a long time to build their trust in a person, which means hours outdoors. Training them is a gradual process because I start by putting the corn in my hand, and lowering my hand to the ground. Each day I raise my hand a little higher. Eventually, my hand is at their eye level and we are face-to-face. This process can take weeks.

While Mrs. Brown and I were in the training process and learning to trust each other, Samantha decided it was a good time to make her presence known. My first thought was to wonder if Samantha would display jealousy at Mrs. Brown eating from my hand. Samantha sauntered over to me to look for her food, and Mrs. Brown walked away. It wasn't long after Samantha started eating when I heard a sound by the trees, and when I glanced over, I saw four babies running toward me. We had seen them all before, but this was the first time that they had appeared together. They walked right up to me, and ate the corn that had fallen on the ground at my feet. A couple of minutes after the babies joined us, a buck came strolling through the trees into my yard.

It was such a peaceful and healing experience, being surrounded by these beautiful wild animals. I am very careful around them because I know enough to know that anything can happen to make them react. I feel so blessed that these marvelous animals know that they are welcome and that they don't have to fear us. It took time, patience, and a whole lot of sunlight to get to where we were hosts to all the deer.

Chapter 4:

Searching for Your Fountain of

Healing

- Have you ever dreamed about boarding a plane, a cruise liner, or a train to visit destinations on your bucket list?

- Have you considered purchasing a retired school bus and turning it into a motor home?

- Have you thought about packing up your car and following the tumbleweeds as you cross state lines?

- Are you a homebody who prefers to visit local places?

There are no right or wrong answers. You will always find a place that fills you with the peace and calm your troubled and weary soul needs. We know that the loss of a loved one affects everyone differently—no one will ever dispute that. My grieving process is different from yours, and yours may be different from what your best friend is experiencing. Your grief may chase you to places where you believe that you'll find the salve to heal your broken heart. My grief may have me walking along the banks of the lake and watching the ducks play in the calm waters. Our grief may cross paths as we go in search of the healing we desire. Some may find their healing habitat sooner than others, and many may have to search a little longer and a little harder.

I have heard people share their experiences when trying to cope with grief. Some have said that they went to visit family in other states. Others have said that they felt the calling to visit other countries. One of my interviewees told me that they had a very difficult time mourning the loss of their father. They applied for a working job in another country, and boarded the plane faster than they could pack their bags. They arrived at their destination and discovered that they were miserable, and that nothing was as advertised, or promised, during the interview process. It took patience, perseverance, and a very thick skin to find another job opportunity. They followed their heart, and it led them to a place where they knew that they had arrived at their version of paradise.

Not everyone has the means, or the inclination, to travel too far from their roots. There are no definitive rules that tell you what you should or shouldn't be doing. One person said that you have to do what is right for you, because you will never find what you're looking for if you are trying to replicate what others do. I believe that person hit it out of the ballpark, because you can't experience someone else's grief. You can't slide into their bodies and take over their feelings. Grief is something that everyone experiences for themselves. We may understand what it is like to grieve or mourn the loss of a loved one, but there is no way that I will ever know the level of pain someone else is carrying in their mind, body, or soul.

I have previously mentioned that everyone grieves in their own way and at their own pace. Some people will run, while others will hang back. You don't need a timetable or a schedule to grieve. I spoke to someone in passing, and they told me that grief doesn't have an expiration date. I didn't pay attention to their comment until I started writing these books; and, the more I think about it, the more I understand that I may never get over my grief, *BUT* I can find ways to help me cope. I have found that writing, reading, and researching has helped me build a coping module that may or may not resonate with everyone.

Destinations Unknown: Finding Ways to Heal Your Grieving Heart

I have to admit that I love doing research for the books I write. Yes, 90% of the books are all about my experiences and my ideas. The other 10% is me making sure I add in some factual information to ensure that I am on the right track—it holds me accountable for what I'm sharing. I learn something new with each book that I write. When I started writing this chapter, I learned something new—a new term that I hadn't heard before: "grief traveler." Looking back and connecting the dots, I never realized that grief traveler was a term that someone had coined when I shared my interviewees' travel experience after the passing of their father.

I have been introduced to two types of people when doing research for this chapter. On the one hand, we have those who enjoy traveling and who have been bitten by the wanderlust bug. They are the ones who are, we can say, running away to *find themselves* and will eventually return to their roots with the answer they had been seeking. They may also be running toward something, but they will eventually tumble their way back to their roots with the answers and peace they were searching for. On the other hand, we have those who prefer to stay close to their roots. They are the ones who are afraid to make drastic changes that will alter the protection they have built around themselves. These are the people who set the pace for their healing and coping strategies. They will make small changes that won't impact their daily lives too much, but it will help them find the healing they need. I believe that they think that slow and steady wins the prize.

No one should be telling you how to grieve, or cope with, the loss of a dearly departed. I have listened to people ramble on about friends or family members who have lost all sense of responsibility after the loss of a loved one, or that they were self-obsessed and thinking of their own needs. I want to say something in defense of everyone, even the ramblers, but I have had to bite my tongue because there is no way to reason with someone when they don't see or understand what others are going through. Everyone needs a cooling-off period and a safe corner, to think about each other's point of view. There is no right or wrong, and when it comes to grief and coping, there never will be. Let's take a look at why the grief "runners" need to break free from their cages and understand why, and how, vacations will help them in the long term.

Running Into the Open Arms of Healing

I have found that the get-up-and-go part of *grief traveling* is a spur-of-the-moment getaway or escape. I have spoken to many of my interviewees who have been wearing their running shoes for years, months, or weeks as they watch their loved ones go through the various stages of their illnesses. Some have told me that their loved ones passed without ever being sick; one moment they were having a cup of coffee and the next they were gone. The thing about death is that no one knows when it will creep up on you. God is the only one who knows when we will be called home. I have always believed that, on the day we are born, God has already selected the day, date, and time that He will come back for us. This is one of those stark reminders that we are not in control of our lives. We are on loan to this world, and we are given a temporary body that has been entrusted to us to fulfill a destiny of God's choice. You won't know what your destiny is, but you do know that you have to do the best you can with what you are given.

Visiting various places or destinations may be part of your destiny. Your grief may be leading you to a place where you are meant to help someone with something they are facing. You may be prompted to start a travel blog for your community, to document your journey through loss and grief. You may have been led to a specific location that has a significant meaning to the life and love of your dearly departed. There are so many hidden questions and answers between the layers of the cloak of grief that we choose to ignore, because we want to block out the pain of losing our loved ones.

Be bold and uncloak yourself for a couple of hours a day, while you are traveling or visiting places. Allow yourself to experience the pain of healing. I do believe that healing from a loss is painful, because it is a reminder that you have to walk through life without your loved one by your side, or a reminder that they are no longer at the other end of the telephone. You don't have to be afraid to heal. You have a support system that is waiting for you to tumble your way back into their lives. I am here for you, too—a virtual stranger who has been where you are—confused, broken, and wanting more.

Grief traveling is not only about hopping on a plane or boarding a cruise liner. You may dedicate a weekend to traveling around your town, county, or state to visit some local places. I have previously mentioned that not everyone has the means to travel the world or take a leave of absence from work to deal with bereavement. I have also mentioned that many people prefer to stick closer to their roots for personal reasons. Grief traveling is when you are visiting places that invite you to remember your feelings, and it helps you navigate your way through the layers of grief.

Your Virtual Travel Guide: The World Is Your Oyster

You don't need a prescription to find healing. You don't need anyone's permission to explore the world or your own backyard. You don't even need a passport or an airplane ticket. You don't need anything extravagant to help you find what you are looking for. It doesn't matter where in the world you find yourself living; I can assure you that you will always find places to explore or re-explore. You will know, if you have been following my journey, that my backyard is my safe haven. It is the place I keep coming back to when my heart feels as if it wants to escape. It is where Amadeus explored every blade of grass, sniffed every leaf, and marked his territory to let everyone know that this was his property. It is where I was introduced to Samantha, Mrs. Brown, and their extended families. My backyard is where I have found healing, where I am closer to Amadeus and Dad, and where I am surrounded by the healing sounds of nature.

Let's explore the oyster, and learn how the locations may be beneficial to helping you find healing. I am sharing ideas about the different types of options that are available to you. Please remember that the examples I share are not intended to force or sway you to do as I say. The beauty of having free will is that you get to turn everything you see or hear into something that is unique to you and your circumstances.

The Beach

I love the beach. I enjoy taking long walks. I enjoy looking out over the ocean to see where the sky meets the water. I love the sounds of the waves breaking on the sand. I enjoy watching the seagulls playing with each other on the sand, or frolicking in the water. I feel closer to God when I'm at the beach. Sunrises and sunsets are breathtaking. The thought that God has painted those beautiful scenes fills my heart with gratitude. They are God's portraits that are being shared with me and everyone else who sees them. You may not share my love for the beach, and that is perfectly okay with me. I have my annoyances, such as the sand. It inserts itself into every crevice and fold of my body and clothing. Romantic picnics are not really beach-friendly, because I often find myself consuming more sand than actual food.

The beach may not be everyone's idea of peace and calm. I'm not suggesting an island vacation, but the key point is that the beach (or any body of water) brings healing and restoration to your soul. I stumbled across an article that highlights the mental health benefits of visiting and spending time at the beach. I like to think that spending time at the beach, or any large body of water, will assist with overall mental health and well-being. It may fill your weary spirit with the peace it yearns for. Let's take a look at some of the points that may potentially help you open that grief cage that you have been hiding away in:

- Break the monotony of your surroundings; the stress of being in the same place day in and day out takes a toll on your health.

- Experience new sights, sounds, scenes, and smells; teach yourself to relax and open your mind to new experiences.

- Sun kisses help with relaxation.

- Feeling the cool breeze on your sun-kissed skin is a reminder that you are alive.

- Practice some water sports such as surfing, wakeboarding, swimming, or paddleboarding.

Spend time with yourself. Take walks along the beach, river, or lake. Talk to God, Mother Nature, or your dearly departed as if they were with you on your stroll. Nature doesn't have to be a scary place, and you don't have to imagine the worst based on stories you have read or that have been shared by third-party people who have most likely never spent time at the beach or at the river. Trust that your angel will guide you, and they are waiting for you to make the first move. I know that when I'm sitting out in my backyard looking at the lake and watching the ducks frolic in the shallow waters, and I hear leaves rustle, that Amadeus has popped in for a visit.

The Mountains

Many studies have been conducted to determine how individuals cope with their mental health status. The topic of mental health is something everyone talks about, yet many are reluctant to admit that they may fall into one of the many categories under the umbrella. I personally know of people who avoid the topic because they don't want to walk around with the label over their heads. Others speak out about their struggles, so that they may help those who don't understand what is going on inside their minds, bodies, and souls. Please, if you suspect that you may be struggling with your mental health, reach out to someone or visit your medical professional for help.

Everyone relates to nature in their own unique way. While some people love the sun, surf, and sand, others may prefer being more in touch with nature by camping or hiking in the mountains. Scientists have noted that individuals who relate to nature may be happier, and it also makes them more aware of environmental concerns and sustainability.

What would a trip to the mountains mean for someone who is trying to mend a broken heart? Breathing in fresh mountain air may not be a Band-Aid for the broken heart, but it is an excellent antiseptic (and a step in the right *healing* direction). I do believe that there is something magical and healing about hiking and camping in the mountains. We tend to rely on our devices, which offer virtual trips to the beach, the rivers, or the mountains. I can honestly say that there is no comparison between virtual and real-life experiences. I understand that finances may be tight, but you have options to get out and explore nature without signing your life away.

Let's take a look at what a visit to the great outdoors can do for you, your mental health, and your grieving heart. We will also take a look at ways in which you can use your time to help you find what you are looking for:

- It can create endorphins that will alleviate stress, settle anxiety, and improve moods.

- It's an ideal setting to practice yoga and meditation.

- Symptoms of depression are reduced when presented with picturesque scenery.

- The sights and sounds of nature instill a calming effect on troubled hearts.

- Hiking or biking in the mountains helps with fitness, which allows you to push yourself to reach your potential.

- Overcome mental fatigue or the "I can't do it" slogan that has been your biggest obstacle; I am telling you that you can do anything you set your mind to, so obliterate that obstacle and reach for the stars.

- Disconnect from the world by leaving your devices at home.

- Tap into nature's Wi-Fi, where you have a direct line between you and God.

Happy Locations

The nature bug may have skipped you and landed on someone else. You need to do whatever it is that makes you happy. If your idea of the great outdoors is strolling through your garden, then so be it. Who is anyone to tell you what you should or shouldn't be doing? I have met people who prefer to release their endorphins by participating in indoor activities. Many people have shared their happy locations with me, which I would never have associated with healing or calming until you listen to their reasons. That is when you experience the *aha* moment. Let's take a look to see what others have shared about places that bring them peace, healing, and clarity.

- **visiting libraries:** Some have said that there is nothing more healing to the soul than feeling the pages between your fingers, smelling the old books, and trailing fingers over images—you can't find that level of happiness when reading on a device.

- **visiting churches:** Older chapels in the countryside are inviting, and allow visitors to experience the craftsmanship in the details of the pulpit and the details on the stained windows.

- **visiting cemeteries:** Walking through rows of gravesites, reading the headstones, and mourning the loss of people you never knew may help with one's grief.

- **visiting antique stores or pawn shops:** Walking through other people's treasures helps you understand that you don't have to hold on to every item your loved one left behind—it is okay to let go, which is a healing experience on its own.

You are the only one who knows where your *happy* is. No one knows your dearly departed the way you do. I cannot stress it enough that you should do whatever it is that makes you happy. Uncloaking yourself for five, ten, or twenty minutes a day, to do something that makes you feel like smiling, is a step in the right direction. I guess this is a good place to tell you that every five, ten, or twenty minutes that you spend uncloaked is a gold medal moment for you, because you are moving in a positive direction.

Your Virtual Travel Guide: Sharing My Happy Places

Life through my eyes is not always as clear as it should be. I have moments where I feel that I am not doing enough to deal with my grief. Other times, I feel as if every eye in the world is watching me while I slink further into my cloak of grief. I have to remind myself that I don't answer to anyone about my feelings. I am very lucky and privileged to have an amazing support system that helps me in more ways than they could ever know. I want to share some thoughts that I have dancing around in my head. I am hoping that my thoughts may help you on your journey to find your peace and happiness.

I have found that certain places make me feel relaxed, at peace, and calm. Have you ever wondered why these places may have such an effect? I have found, during my research, that places I find peaceful and calming don't affect everyone else. The simple answer may be that no two people are alike—as has been mentioned more than a couple of times. Our brains are not wired to act, or react, to a situation in the same way that it does to your partner or best friend. Some people find joy in taking their dogs for a walk, and others enjoy sitting on a bench in the park reading a book or watching people ride bikes and throw balls. You can be feeding the ducks at the lake, or visiting a conservation area where you get to learn about the natural habitat of rescued animals. The onus is on you to find your happy place. This chapter has shown you that you don't have any limits, and if you want to spend your day sitting in the backyard, you can do just that. If you want to drive up to the mountains and lie on the bed of your truck to look up at the dark, starry skies, you should do it. Any place that brings you peace and calm, and makes you feel as if you are closer to your dearly departed, is the happiest place you will ever be. I have found that sitting outside at night, looking up at the moon and the stars, and spotting a shooting star helps me to realize how small we (humans) are, and how vast the heavens are. My favorite place may not be yours, which is perfectly fine.

One of my favorite places to visit is a church—the older, the better. When I lived in the United Kingdom, I would go out of my way to sit in an old church where I found peace and quiet. This would be an ideal setting to practice yoga and meditation because it is so peaceful. You can almost feel as if your soul is leaving your body. You think about so many things, and you feel waves of peace and calm roll over you as the stress of life washes away. I love the smells of old churches. I run my fingers over the original pews. I am held captive by the way the sun shines through the stained windows and the inside of the church explodes with colors. The peace and calm of the church are intensified by the sound of Gregorian chant music playing in the background. I believe that the church holds many memories for me that date back to when I was an altar boy who didn't know what grief was and who had no worries. It was a time when everyone in my family was still young, alive, and well.

A Youthful Memory

I purchased my first motorcycle in the late '90s to commute to work. I'd had my bike for approximately three months when I chatted to one of my senior managers at the watercooler. I had just changed into my leathers and was heading out. He told me that he had been riding motorcycles for over 30 years. He shared his experience (and fears) with me as he explained that riding is one of the strangest experiences because it is both exciting and dangerous. One has to be aware at all times and pay close attention to the road and the surface conditions, watch out for other cars, take the weather conditions into account, and keep an eye out for animals and pedestrians. My senior manager shared his experience with me, but ended by saying that there was something equally peaceful about riding a motorcycle and feeling the freedom when out on the open road.

Everyone needs to know and understand that everything in life comes with risks. I didn't understand why he shared his experience with me until a couple of months later. He was right. You are surrounded by danger, yet you feel at peace on your bike. Maybe it is because you are wearing a helmet. The pressure of the air around you is minimized by the protection your helmet gives you, and you can only hear the sound of your breathing, the blood rushing through your veins, or the sound of your heart bouncing against your ribcage. I would like to invite you to replicate this experience under my guidance. Cup your hands over your ears and block out the sounds around you. Take a deep breath, exhale slowly, and breathe normally. You can hear your heart beating, the sound of your breathing (when calm), and a swishing sound as the blood flows through your veins. Your body produces those calming sounds, and it is also what many medical professionals stress on patients who have anxiety—ground yourself by focusing on the sounds coming from your body.

A Youthful Memory Continued

I owned my motorcycle for many years. One of my favorite pastimes was riding to the Lake District in the northwest of England. The Lake District was best known for its hills, mountains, and gorgeous countryside and lanes. With its small towns and villages, it is truly one of the most beautiful areas I have ever visited. I do believe that there were more sheep than people in this area. One of the first things I would do when visiting my happy places is find a place where I could enjoy the scenery and local produce. I rolled into the town of Keswick and found a coffee shop that ticked all the requirements of my visit. I found a spot where I could sit outside and take in the beautiful views. I would order a cup of coffee and a home-baked oatmeal raisin cookie. I would find myself people-gazing, and was always mesmerized by the happiness I could see on people's faces. Why wouldn't they be happy? They are living in some of the most beautiful areas in all of England. The Lake District, an hour away from Liverpool, was breathtakingly gorgeous.

I would utilize my time visiting this area by thinking about everything. Whatever topic popped into my mind would be hashed out between me and my brain until we reached a compromise. I can tell you that there is nothing better than arguing with yourself, and finding a resolution that suits you both—yes, me and the voices in my head have a beautiful relationship. I will admit that these types of interactions or thoughts occur in certain places such as when I'm out exploring the countryside, visiting a church, staring out the window during a rainstorm, riding my bike, or sitting in the park.

Everyone has to find their special place that speaks to them. Find a place where you can be one with the nature that calls your name. I have shared many examples to give you an idea of what you may be looking for. You may not like the quiet and solitude, and maybe attending an open-air concert is more your scene. This is your chance to find something that resonates with you, your mood, and your level of grief. Think about your loved ones who have passed on, and imagine a place where you would feel closer to them. Remember that the sky's the limit. Imagine what your loved ones are doing, and don't ever be afraid to speak to them as if they were with you in their physical form.

Chapter 5:

Using the Great Outdoors to

Cope With Grief

Many of the people I have spoken to have said that it was beneficial to them to stay busy during times of grief. The "downtime" you experience, in the period after the passing of a loved one and the funeral, drags on for what seems like forever. I remember that I kept busy by doing odds and ends around the house for Mum. I strongly believe that this "downtime" sees you high on adrenaline and not wanting to experience that crash and burn you hear about. I guess you could say that the hero complex makes an appearance and you don't want to be seen falling apart. You have to constantly remind yourself that you can break down when you return to "normal" life. Yes, normal is a word I have forgotten the meaning of. How do you find normal after the loss of a loved one? The short answer is that you don't. Instead, you create a *new* normal that centers around life without your loved one.

A team of researchers conducted a study to evaluate whether physical outdoor activities assist during the grieving period. They surmised that grief is something that occurs naturally, and no one goes out to find it. Many people develop anxiety and depression during their time of grief. The purpose of the study was to understand whether physical activities aided those who were struggling to come to terms with their bereavement. The study involved a review of different databases which also included studies performed on people of various ages who had experienced the loss of a loved one. The results of the study focused on different types of losses which included the loss of a parent or parents, partners or spouses, child or children, and acquaintances. The physical activities which were used during the study included walking, hiking, running, yoga, and martial arts. It was also recorded that all types of physical activities were beneficial to the participants who were grieving because they allowed them to be free, they could deal with their emotions on their own terms, and they were distracted (Williams et al., 2021).

I don't know about you, but I'm inclined to agree with the researchers that the possibility of participating in physical activities is not such a bad idea. I believe that finding an activity that takes you outdoors and away from everyday distractions, such as digital devices, is what is needed. Don't be afraid to leave your comfort zone. Outdoor activities are not limited to walking, running, or cycling. Don't be afraid to try different activities to find one that is the perfect fit for you. Remember that *you* are looking for activities to help *you* navigate *your* feelings to cope with *your* grief. This book is not about giving you ideas to help family, friends, or acquaintances wade through their grief—it is all about *you*, the most important person in *your* life. I believe that you will find something that will speak healing into your mind, body, and soul. Look and listen for signs and guidance from your dearly departed, about what you could be doing to honor their memory.

Exploring Nature-Based Activities to Soothe a Wounded Heart

I believe that it is safe to say that not everyone likes being outdoors. I can understand that nobody wants to get dirt under their nails, or be attacked by a colony of ruthless mosquitoes when they smell fresh blood. What could be worse than being outside, breathing in the fresh air, and hearing birds sing? I'm not going to tell you what you should be doing, but I am going to ask you to keep an open mind. I cannot stress the importance of exploring or looking at something before you walk away from an idea or a suggestion. I have always believed in trying something at least once before saying that it wasn't something I wanted to pursue.

We are quick to tell our children to play a musical instrument or participate in a sport that they don't want to. They will tell you over and over again that they don't want to do those activities, but you will tell them that they will learn to love them and, eventually, excel at them. It is the same scenario as I explained in Chapter 2 when trying new food and tastes. Do you see a pattern forming here? It is okay for you to lay down the law and tell your children or others what they should be doing. But, here you are, kicking your heels in and refusing to try something because it will challenge you and take you away from your comfort zone. Hey pot, the kettle is calling your black. I am not here to criticize you, but I am here to remind you that you don't have to be afraid to get dirt under your nails or be attacked by a colony of mosquitoes.

This is your invitation to join me, as we explore some of the nature-based activities that I have found. These activities are merely recommendations that offer various benefits to help you on your journey to coping with grief, which includes your mental and physical well-being. Remember to bring your open mind and to leave your comfort zone at the door, where it will be waiting for you when you return.

Equine Healing Therapy

You shouldn't let the size of a horse intimidate you. I know, easier said than done, especially when they tower over you. Growing up, you were always told not to approach a horse from behind, or stand behind them, because their kicks are dangerous. Their size, their flaring nostrils, and their stomping around are enough to fill anyone with fear. That is, until you get to know them and spend time hanging around their paddocks.

These gentle giants demand respect from everyone who enters their safe haven. They are very playful, and like to nudge you when you don't give them the attention they believe that they deserve. They won't intentionally hurt you, unless they are injured and you are not aware or you do something to threaten them. They are mischievous beasts who try to push their luck when they are being lunged or when riders are doing their lessons. They will buck to get attention and, when being scolded, you may see them "laughing" by baring their teeth.

Horses are very intuitive animals. They know when people are afraid, when their owners have had a bad day, or when someone is grieving. You don't have to spend time with them to see how they interact with their human counterparts. I have been in a very privileged position to witness various interactions between people and horses. One of my interviewees shared a story with me that I had to include here. They had started their horse-riding career when they were seven years old, just after a medical diagnosis that plunged them into depression—yes, even children can be diagnosed with depression. One of their friends had a horse farm out in the country, and they approached the parents to ask if they would allow them to offer riding lessons. The parents agreed and everyone jumped into action to make this happen. The owner of the farm reached out to a rescue organization that had a pony that had been rescued. It wasn't long before Rayne, the rescue pony, was introduced to the farm. He was a naughty little guy who believed that he was Houdini in a previous life. His disappearing tricks got him into a lot of trouble. That is, until he was introduced to his person.

Remember that Rayne's new person didn't know about him until they arrived at the farm. Without any hesitation, Rayne ran up to his person, as everyone stood around to watch the interaction. He nudged his new person's hand until it was on his head, and he leaned in while the two just stood there; one cried and the other offered support. My interviewee shared that video with me, which I will admit had me swallowing back tears.

Do I believe that horses help people with their mental and physical well-being? Absolutely, without a doubt. We are quick to shut down suggestions, but we are slow to try new things. Therapists suggest equine therapy to people of all ages. You don't necessarily have to ride horses, but you could lead them around the arena, lunge them, groom them, or wash them down. Spending time at horse farms—whether you are sitting in your car, on a bench, or actively walking around and participating in activities—is guaranteed to lift your spirits and reduce anxiety. Something else that was shared with me was that speaking to the horse helped unload a lot of anger, fear, and heartache that they believed a normal person would not understand. They believed that their horse understood every word that was being said to them. They would find themselves nose-to-nose at the doors of the stable after an unforgettable couple of hours together.

The Healing Powers of Fishing

There are two ways that people can enjoy the great outdoors: as an active participant or as a spectator. I love being outdoors, and I like trying new activities. I may not like everything I try—which is fine because I can say that I tried, I conquered, and it was or wasn't for me. Grief comes with a lot of baggage. You tend to forget how to take care of yourself in the sense that you don't worry about your diet or exercise.

Fishing is one of those activities where you are required to spend time outdoors. I do believe that people are put off by the idea of dressing a hook with worms, pulling the hook out of the fish's mouth, or gutting the fish. This is where you may encounter the wrath of the colony of mosquitoes or their buddies, the nuisance flies. You may also be introduced to a variety of bugs of varying species, shapes, and sizes. You are most likely to encounter some of the elements of nature which are being smothered with kisses from the sun, being seduced by the ripples of the water, and the wisps of wind.

I would like to issue you with an invitation—it could be a one-time invite or an open-ended, repeat invitation. Pack a picnic basket, throw in sunblock and water (to stay hydrated), and head off to a river or lake in your county. The fishing rod, hooks, sinkers, and worms are optional. Find a spot where you have a clear view over the body of water you have chosen. Settle in, and experience nature as you have never done before. I am going to list a couple of the benefits of fishing, which you may find helpful and may want to incorporate on your next adventure to the river or lake:

- **exercise:** You have to use your muscles and strength to get from your vehicle to your spot on the side of the river, stream, or lake, as well as carry everything you need to make your stay comfortable.

- **lungs full of fresh air:** Nature is offering you the best it has to offer—clean air that hasn't been tainted by carbon monoxide and polluted air.

- **strengthening your immune system:** Fishing or sitting on the banks of the river reduces stress levels, which in turn helps lower blood pressure and fills you with peace and calm.

Patience

I felt that patience needed its own little paragraph. Patience is something everyone says they have an abundance of, but when faced with a situation, patience is the first to leave the room. We need to learn how to be kind to ourselves. We have to learn how to trust ourselves. Grief is not something that you can sweep under the mat and hope that it never returns. Grief will be with you until you learn to be patient and understand what you are going through. Patience doesn't require you to do everything right now, because tomorrow is another day. Spend time in the great outdoors; walk around a ranch and meet the animals, watch an angler catching his 100th salmon and cheer him on, go camping in the canyon, or go to a conservation center and feed some rescued animals. Be patient with yourself, and trust that you will find the healing you require.

How Nature-Based Activities Help Me

I have found that life doesn't stand still because I am grieving. Life isn't too bothered about my feelings or what I am going through. We can't expect the world, or life, to stop because we are mourning the loss of our loved ones. I have previously mentioned that the normal life we once identified no longer exists, and it is up to each one of us to create a new normal. We need to learn how to cope with our grief and embrace the new normal, without any instructions. This is one of those life lessons where you learn by living, and live by learning.

I would be one of the first to admit that life doesn't just toss us out on our ears without any guidance. We have our senses, and we have to learn how to use those senses. This is where we trust our brains to guide us. We will be introduced to sights, sounds, feelings, and smells which we have the chance to interpret and mold to our needs. This doesn't have to be a lonely journey. It is an opportunity to expand our vision and rely on the gifts we have been given. We can participate in various activities such as exploring caves, hiking to find waterfalls, or taking art classes in nature. You can do whatever you want to because you are building a life to accommodate you and your healing heart.

This book is all about how nature can help you heal. You may not have liked everything that I have brought to this book, especially recommendations about going hiking or fishing. I had to ask myself a couple of questions to help me understand where I was on my journey—questions such as: *Why do certain nature-related interactions have a specific effect on my mood, health, or soul?* Then there are the animals I am in contact with, and instead of watching them from the safety of my home where I am protected, I have the intense desire to be outside and move among them. I spend much of my time in the great outdoors because that is where I feel free. I ride my bike. I feed Samantha, Mrs. Brown, and their families. I am visited by ducks who come, en-masse, from the lake to see what they are missing out on in the food department. I enjoy taking trips to the mountains whenever I have time.

I recently took a drive to the mountains in Georgia, where I went panning for gold. I found approximately two dollars' worth of gold. Finding gold was a fun activity, but for me, it was about being in the mines. We were probably 200 feet underground, and it reminded me of Dad. I had a memory flashback to 1977, when I was about 11 years old, and we went on a family vacation to Cornwall—a county in the southwest of

England. It is the most beautiful coastal town with stunning beaches. Surfers from across the globe would descend on the Cornwall beaches at certain times of the year. It was on this vacation that Dad decided to go and explore one of the old tin mines in Cornwall. It wasn't so much a tour as it was an actual working expedition. Dad would go down the tin mine with a group of other men and a guide.

Dad and the other men were taught how to mine for tin, and they would work for several hours. Mum was terrified and worried about Dad being gone all night. She would only show signs of being relaxed when he returned in the early hours of the next morning. This is the memory that came to my mind while I was down in the gold mines of the Georgia mountains. I felt as if Dad was with me, smiling and reminding me of his time in the tin mines in 1977. I'm not going to lie and tell you that I wasn't intimidated about being 200 feet underground, because I was. I may have been slightly more than freaked out, but I felt a calmness wash over me when I remembered Dad and his Cornwall mining experience because I knew, without a shadow of a doubt, that Dad was right there beside me.

It is moments like this, doing something and being somewhere you wouldn't normally be, that help with the grieving process. Here is another one of my invitations to try something new. Think of something your loved one enjoyed doing, and go out and replicate it. If they loved hiking in the mountains to go bird watching, you can head off to the bird park and spend time looking at the birds. Arm yourself with a notebook, a camera, or anything you would need to capture your nature moment, and go out there and build new memories. Use your senses to see, hear, smell, feel, or taste your surroundings. Allow nature to envelop you in the biggest embrace you have ever experienced, and feed off the healing powers that are being shared with you.

Chapter 6:

Finding the Author Within

Yourself

Writing was one of my best kept secrets. It was a place where I could express myself without speaking out loud. Growing up in the dinosaur era, we didn't have the technology we have now. I would use my pocket money to buy notebooks or journals, and stock up on pens and pencils. Everything I needed could fit in my backpack. I knew that I could go anywhere, pull out my journal and pens, and write to my heart's content. I would write about anything that popped into my mind. If I saw a bird drinking nectar out of a flower, I would create a short story about it. You have no limitations when you are writing, and no one is going to judge you, because you are the gatekeeper to your most personal thoughts.

I have spoken to many people who have said that they could never write because they can't string two words together. I have found that, when you think about what you are doing, you do find yourself struggling. I call that "performance anxiety" because you are trying too hard. The words will flow when you forget about why you are writing. The problem with humans is that we try too hard. We need to hit the pause button, and think about why we do what we do. I have found, especially over the last couple of years, that writing has been therapeutic for me. Don't worry about the writer's block you encounter because it is one of those necessary roadblocks that tells you to stop, take a couple of steps back, and re-strategize where you want to go.

Scientists and researchers have joined forces with therapists and grief counselors, to put together a study to prove that journaling helps individuals cope with grief, stress, or trauma. The Harvard Medical School's health department has noted that writing is beneficial to strengthening one's immune system, because it relieves stress and improves the mood of the individual. I do believe that it is safe to assume that we agree with the professionals that holding onto residual anger, anxiety, stress, or frustration has negative effects on our overall mental and physical health and well-being. Many therapists who work with trauma victims recommend that their patients keep a journal, which helps assess their mental health (Harvard Health Publishing, 2016).

Learning How to Manage Your Grief

We know that grief is something we can't control. It comes and goes like a thief in the night. One moment you are feeling happy, and the next you are struggling to breathe, as the sadness and longing for your loved one overwhelms you. Writing, in my opinion, is one of the best remedies to help ease the side effects of grief. Some people find it more difficult to put their grief into words, and this is another one of those situations where I believe that writing helps. Many of the studies that have been conducted by therapists, grief counselors, scientists, and researchers have agreed that writing is healing for the soul. However, we have to understand that we don't all grieve the same way. I may find that writing is healing and therapeutic, but someone else may find that it's daunting, it's stressful, and leads to memories they don't want to face.

One thing about journaling I need to point out is that it is your *personal* guide. No one is going to see your thoughts unless you share them with others. Whatever you write in your journal stays private, so you don't have to be afraid of holding back your thoughts. If you want to write about the memories you would rather forget; it would be a good idea to extract them from your mind, onto paper, where you never have to read them again—unless you want to revisit your past sometime in the future. I have found that when I extract the words from my mind, I have room for new memories and adventures. Everything I treasure most about my time with Dad and Amadeus is in my heart. My heart holds everything together, and that is why I find it easier to transform my memories into words so that I can choose to either share them or save them to share with future generations.

Let's take a look at some points shared by the Harvard Medical School's medical professionals who share their thoughts and experiences about how journaling may help you process grief.

- Allow yourself to feel the different emotions when writing—sadness, anger, frustration, or happiness.

- Writing allows you to let go of all your feelings; you don't have to hold back on your feelings, because it is your journey.

- Keep your writing consistent; write something each day—even if it is one or two words a day; you are learning a new habit and consistency is important.

Journaling Is For Everyone

I was recently reminded that journaling doesn't necessarily mean extracting the words from your mind, allowing them to flow through your fingers and onto paper (or the screen). Journaling may involve doodling, sketching, or simply outlining dreams and desires for future projects. I think it would be safe to say that you and I don't know each other. We've never met, yet you know more about me than what I know about you— right? I'm sharing myself with you and the rest of the world because my writing career was inspired by my journaling. I wanted to, and chose to, share my grief with everyone because I realized that people don't like sharing the vulnerable side of themselves. Everyone has this urge to portray the sunshine and roses in their lives. Life is about taking risks, like putting your heart and soul out there to be shown some love and kindness, or to be trodden on.

I did a little digging in the dusty archives of the world wide web, and found something that reminded me that this regular

Liverpudlian guy, living in one of the most beautiful places in the United States (I'm biased), joined the ranks of "famous" who journaled. However, these people didn't really write as much as what they doodled, sketched, and designed.

- Leonardo da Vinci is believed to have over 7,000 pages of drawings, diagrams, and notes in sketchbooks.

- Frida Kahlo, a Mexican artist, journaled her physical disabilities by capturing her struggles in over 70 watercolors in her diary (Wolfe, 2020).

You may not be an artist, and have no inclination to design anything, so why still peddle the idea of journaling? I am so happy that you have raised this question, and I would love to share my version of why "normal" people should journal. This is one of those "did you know" moments when I ask you if you knew that "famous" people journaled. It is very true. I stumbled across a couple of names of celebrities who have mentioned that they journaled their thoughts. I do believe that this is where I remind you that journaling is something that everyone can benefit from. You never know where it may lead you if you don't try, so before you put up your cautionary roadblocks to drown me out, allow me to introduce you to:

- Oprah Winfrey: a famous talk show hostess and actress

- Warren Buffe: business magnate, investor, and philanthropist

- Josh Waitzkin: chess player and martial artist

- Richard Branson: a British entrepreneur who founded the Virgin Group, which is an umbrella corporation for the airline, radio stations, hotels, and gyms across the world

- Lady Gaga: world-famous singer, actress, and songwriter

Let's continue on this journey to see how journaling may benefit you on your road to healing.

The Benefits of Journaling

I have touched on some of the benefits of journaling based on studies by medical professionals. I wanted to keep the momentum alive, especially after presenting you with examples of famous or well-known people who you didn't know. I do believe that their journaling status would have remained unknown to the general public if journalists hadn't asked them specific types of questions such as:

- What keeps you grounded when you are working on big projects?

- How do you unwind after a difficult day at the office?

- What motivates you to keep doing what you do?

- How do you cope with the loss of your loved one?

Yes, these are the types of questions I would imagine were being asked. You could ask yourself these questions, too, to see whether journaling may be something you should be doing. I would like to present you with a couple of choices. One of the choices is that you can stay hidden between the layers of the cloak of grief. The other choice is that you can permit yourself to have a guilt-free experience, thanks to journaling. I'm not going to put you on the spot and force you to choose one, the other, or both of the choices. Follow along to see what the benefits may be. Don't be too surprised when something jumps out at you, grabs you by the cheeks, and helps you realize that this is something you might enjoy.

How Can Journaling Help You Cope With Grief?

I have found that, when you are hit square in the chest with life-changing news, that you are instantly cloaked by a mental block. You lose focus, and you feel as if you are on a roundabout that won't stop spinning. You feel as if you have been sucked into a giant hole as you try to understand what is happening. I felt like that when Dad let me know that he had been diagnosed with cancer. I needed to find the first flight to the UK because I needed to be with Dad. We did go over and spend a week with him. Upon our return to the United States, we had a certain pandemic strike lock us in and toss the key away, while we tried to understand what was happening. It is during this time of uncertainty that you are left with your thoughts. The *what ifs*, *whys*, *whens*, *hows*, and all the other unasked questions start seeping into your subconscious, and you are left feeling as if there is a giant, gaping hole staring at you. This is where journaling can help you identify where you are in the healing process. Writing can help you in many ways which include:

- making sense of your feelings

- slowing down and thinking about your next moves

- remembering the finer details of your loved one such as your favorite scent, food, colors, or flowers

- a safe place to express your thoughts without judgment or condemnation

These points have been mentioned multiple times, but I do believe that a refresher is always welcomed. We may see or hear something that goes in one ear and flies out the other ear, without sticking around; but, if you are reminded, you are more likely to remember something crucial that is beneficial to your story.

Choosing a Journal

Being a child in the '70s was much easier than it is in the 2000s (in my opinion). We didn't have the distractions today's children have. We had a couple of options growing up, but not nearly as many as children today have. We didn't have hundreds of television channels to choose from, and we watched whatever Mom and Dad were watching, which was mostly the news and some of Dad's black-and-white cowboy films. I previously mentioned that I would take my pocket money, head off to the store, and buy some notebooks, pens, and pencils which were perfect for journaling. I didn't know that there were different options, and I didn't have to think about why I wanted to journal. I just wanted a book to write my thoughts in. I needed to make room for more thoughts, so I used whatever was available to me at the time.

You may not have liked my method of journaling or the process I went about to start my writing journey, which is perfectly fine. I found an article that was more than forthcoming with ideas to help those who struggle to make choices. I would like to remind you that journaling is not necessarily a pen and paper hobby, but that it could also be done on your digital device of choice. I am in no position to tell you that you have to choose one or the other, because each of the options means something different to each person. Some people may choose to journal by starting a blog or through a secure online portal, and others may choose to buy proper hardcover journals. This is a hobby that has no right or wrong way, and you have the creative freedom to do whatever you see fit. What are some of the choices you need to make when deciding on the right fit?

- What size journal are you looking at—normal, small, compact, or a sketchbook size?

- Are you looking for detailed pages with dates, patterns, affirmations, or writing prompts?

- What purpose is your journal meant to represent?

Whatever you choose is what is going to be perfect for you. Remember that the choices you make are yours alone, and the journey of journaling is not going to be influenced by the people around you. Journaling is meant to give you a safe place to be real, open, and raw with your feelings and emotions.

The Effects Journaling Had on Me as a Child and Adult

We live in a digital age where everything is online. I believe, as I always have, that everyone has a right to do whatever they want to. It is not my job to come in here and tell you that you need to do this, that, and the other. I can share my opinions, thoughts, and ideas with you—which I have been doing—but I am not going to force you to do something you are not comfortable with. I know that many people find themselves standing at a crossroads and don't know which way to go. Many may find themselves looking for inspiration, and others may need a nudge.

I have many thoughts when it comes to journaling. I will be the first to admit that journaling is not easy. You go through periods—possibly even years—where you avoid journaling. I spoke to someone who wrote and journaled for many years, until something traumatic happened and they deserted their journals. They had a journal, sometimes more than one, in every room of their apartment. They showed me a photo of their journals, and I may have counted 18 or 19 different journals in all shapes, sizes, and formats. I asked them why they stopped writing, and they told me that they lost a vital role player in their journaling journey—the loss of a parent. Call me confused, but I thought people turned to writing to help them with their grief; but, it turns out that grieving can also cause writer's block so that someone can stop writing for eight very long years. They tried to write again. They would sit with one of the many journals for up to 30 minutes per day and only write one or two sentences—on a good day.

They spoke about sitting out in the garden, under their umbrella trees, and thinking that they would write a couple of pages. Nothing would happen. It wasn't until they had a dream in which their parent spoke to them and told them that they were wasting a gift that had been handpicked, by God, for them. The dream was so real that they believed their parent had been there, but running through the apartment showed no signs of anyone other than them in the home. They saw one of the newer journals on the chest of drawers, and they knew that their writer's block had been lifted. They spent the following three hours writing and remembering every little detail about their loved one. They captured everything they had stored in their mind palace for eight years, and emptied the vault to make room for more memories. I asked them, out of curiosity, what they were planning to do with their journals; I was told that they would never see the light of day, because it was memories for their younger family members who needed to be introduced to their dearly departed loved ones.

Journaling My Journey

I previously mentioned that writing has helped me far beyond my expectations. I enjoyed writing, but I only had a couple of journals. I remember documenting my move to the United States. It was a harrowing journey that saw me uprooting my life to move to another country, with an eight-year-old in tow. I started writing my moving journal to help me remember what I was thinking, and documented my thoughts. If you have ever moved—whether it is from one home to another, one state to another, or one country to another—you would understand the amount of stress you carry around with you. Writing that journal helped me stay sane, and it was a way for me to share my thoughts with myself. I still have that journal, and I will bring it out when nostalgia hits me, but reading it now seems so surreal.

I wrote that journal as a youngster, and reading it now reminds me that I have matured over the years. What I had written may not make a lot of sense to someone else reading it, but it reminds me of where I was, and how far I have come. I recall that I was worried about the massive changes I was inflicting upon myself and Jessica, when in reality, it was a leap of faith. I can't remember why I was so worried about moving, as I look back on my thoughts today. I believe that time does change a person, not completely, but looking back you can see growth.

I recently found another journal that I had created to document a trip I took to Portugal in 2008. Mum, Dad, Gillian, Stephen, and their two children went to Portugal on a "walk down memory lane" holiday. Mum was born in Portugal, and at the age of seven, moved with my grandparents to England. I decided to join up with my family in the town where Mum was born. It was the most amazing two weeks we spent together as a family. My journal was filled with so many funny moments. I had filled my journal with photos and lots of writing because I wanted to remember everything. It is nice having the images, but it is even better to read what is written after many years. It awakens the nostalgia, and you are transported back in time as you imagine walking through the towns, markets, and visiting places. You can almost hear the laughter, feel the weather on your skin, and smell the air as you remember that specific instance you are reading about. An emotion goes far deeper than any photograph could ever express.

Journaling Advice

I wanted to end this chapter by sharing some advice to those who are new to the world of journaling. Before you turn to your digital device to capture your feelings, or emotions, consider the "old school" route. There is just something special about putting your pen onto a piece of paper that awakens some senses you may not have realized are there. The smell of the paper and the ink just transports you to another world. Take a walk through the stationary department at Target or

Walmart, and look at their journals. You are presented with many different choices. The paper in one journal may be different in another one. Allow your senses to guide you. Take your time, and find one that works for you.

Alternatively, you could do some research to help you find a journal that will be the right fit, with the type of pen you want to choose. Some pens don't blot as well as others, and others will smudge a little more when your hand accidentally brushes over the words. Find a pen that will write smoothly. I recently purchased a fountain pen for less than $20, which I have found enhances my writing experience. It just makes me want to write more.

You can start focusing on the finer details of writing once you have been outfitted with the perfect journal and pen for you. Something I have told people who have asked for advice is that *what* and *when* you write is not as important as *being prepared* with your journal. Carry it around with you, or keep it in your car, because you will never know when inspiration will strike you. Always be prepared, and listen out for that perfect word, phrase, or paragraph that will inspire you.

Chapter 7:

An Open Invitation—Viewing Religious Beliefs Through My Eyes

I have found that it is impossible to please everyone. When you find yourself being one of over seven billion people in the world, you realize that the person standing beside you may not share your opinions. I have done the unthinkable, and that was to read comments on posts made on the different social media platforms. Some comments are heartwarming where posters are praying for strength and guidance, and others are blaming God for whatever tragedy has happened. I have found that social media, in general, has become a cesspool of toxicity.

- When did humanity lose focus of its creator?

- Why are people seeing religion as a threat?

- Why are people so angry all the time?

I wish I had the answers to these questions and many more like them. I am not a mind reader, and I cannot speak for everyone else. I am not here to force my beliefs on you or anyone else. I have experienced trauma and hardships, and I have had my moments when I shot up some angry prayers, demanding answers. We all go through those moments, and guess what—God was, and always will be, 10 steps ahead of us. God loved you when he created you, He loved you when you turned your back on Him, and He will welcome you back with open arms when you find your way back to Him.

Do you remember what I asked of you when we set out on this journey? I asked you to keep an open mind. I am going to ask you again to keep an open mind, and I am also going to ask you to be respectful of my beliefs. I am not going to judge, condemn, or bully you because you don't share my beliefs. My other books may be all the evidence you need to prove that I have an open mind. My books are a welcome portal to people from all walks of life, which includes religions. Please join me on the last leg of our journey together. We are hurtling toward the end, and I felt the need to share something very near and dear to my heart.

Using Religion to Cope With Grief

I know and understand that we come from different backgrounds, and everyone is raised according to their familial beliefs. It is no secret that I was raised in the Catholic faith; I speak about it in all my books. I even went through a stage where I wanted to become a priest, but I guess God had other plans for me. I have met people from different religions who have shared their beliefs with me. I have met people who don't believe in God, and they respect my choice as I respect theirs. Life is too short to fight about something we can't control, and religion is something we can't control. I'm not ashamed to be Catholic or a Christian. I'm not afraid to have friends who are pagans or agnostic. We respect each other's beliefs and know not to force our beliefs on each other.

I have not brought you here to deceive or trick you to believe in my beliefs. A good portion of this book has been about utilizing the gifts that God created for us—those gifts that we have taken for granted. We don't take the time to appreciate those remarkable gifts because we are always running around and doing things to make life easier for us. This book is being written to help you slow down and think about the gifts you take for granted. This book acts as a reminder that life is short, grief is real, and we are human beings with emotions and feelings. We have all found ourselves here because we have something in common. We are here to navigate our way through the cloak of grief after losing our loved ones. Like it or not, religion is part of a parcel you may not want to think about, but it is something that helps many. It may not help you right now, as you deal with the stages of grief, but one day you may find it helpful.

Read the Bible Every Day

Did you know that the Bible is an all-in-one book that covers just about every niche and genre in the modern-day market? The Bible consists of 66 books, and in those books you will find drama, murder, mystery, science fiction, romance, adventure, and comedy. The Bible is also an excellent source offering lessons in geography, history, environmental studies, poetry, songs, and biographies. Not only does the Bible present you with so much content, but it also offers you many different versions, depending on what you prefer. I like to keep things simple, so you will find me sharing Bible verses from the New International Version (NIV).

Are you one of those individuals who doesn't know where to start when picking up a Bible? I can guarantee that you are not alone. I have met with many people who have told me that they know Bible verses, but they have never read the Bible from start to finish. I have had others tell me that they have tried to read the Bible, but lose interest. I stumbled across an article that answered a pressing question as to the benefits of reading the Bible. I hope that the following list of examples will help you make a decision that is right for you.

- You can hear God speaking into your life.

- You will experience your *aha* moment when you read something that you have been asking.

- You will experience peace, calm, and upliftment.

- You will learn how to interpret your destiny.

- You will learn about God's gifts, and how to apply them to your life.

- You will learn to trust God with all minor and major decisions in your life.

- You will grow in strength and courage.

- You will learn to distinguish between right and wrong.

The Bible has so many hidden treasures between the verses that we ignore or choose not to acknowledge. You have a choice whether you want to read the Bible or not. One thing that I noticed during the pandemic that swept across the globe is that many people bought into the religious business. Conspiracy theorists all but said that the rapture was upon us, and everyone was hurrying to find their salvation. One thing I can tell you is that God doesn't want us to be afraid of death. I have previously said that we are on loan to this world. The bodies we find ourselves in are a temporary home for our souls. Genesis 2:7 tells us: "Then the Lord God formed a man from the dust of the ground and breathed into his nostrils the breath of life, and the man became a living being."

What Does Reading the Bible Do for You?

One of my interviewees told me that they received their first Bible when they were 10 years old. They sent me images of the Bible, which have trebled in size because it is filled with bookmarks and pieces of paper with verses on them. A flip-through shows a very colorful interior with highlighted verses and passages of importance, and even more images of handwritten notes, to remind the next generation of everything they should study and focus on. Seeing the images of this Bible reminded me that we live in the digital age where we can't feel the pages, make notes, or even highlight important verses. I would suggest that you invest in a handheld version of the Bible, one that you can customize to your liking, and still be stylish enough to catch the eye of curious onlookers.

A 2016 study conducted by the University of Utah School of Medicine saw researchers study the brain activity of participants who were praying and reading their Bibles. The scientists detected that three areas of the brain were most active during these activities. Furthermore, scientists determined that dopamine—a chemical in the brain—was released into the body. It is believed that the release of dopamine contributed to participants being more focused, happy, and motivated when reading the Bible (Ferguson, 2016).

If scientists and researchers are showing evidence of what reading the Bible can do for a person, who are we to argue? Again, I am not here to tell you what to do. This is your decision, and I'll still care for you regardless of the path you decide to take.

Coping With Grief: Turn to the Bible

I have presented you with many different types of advice, tips, and activities that would help you find peace during your time of grief. I have shared stories and experiences, and I have even given you a glimpse of my faith. We know that grief doesn't come with a list of instructions that tells us what we should do. Everything we experience is led by our emotions which, as you know, are very sensitive and slightly unreliable. Grief doesn't discriminate against who it will consume. Many don't even know they are being affected by grief until they find themselves in a position where they cannot control their emotions. I observed a mother and her son at the store some time ago. The son, probably about five or six years old, seemed to be angry and wouldn't listen to his mother. She dropped to her haunches in front of him and told him that it was okay to cry and that he didn't need to be angry all the time. The son looked at her with shock and horror all over his face and loudly exclaimed that "cowboys don't cry!" At that, he turned away from her and stomped off. The mother stood up and the tears flowed from her eyes as she watched her son walk away.

I wish I had told the son that cowboys do cry, and it is not a sign of weakness to cry. I'm not ashamed to show my emotions, because I have nothing to hide. I cry for Dad and Amadeus. Someone once told me that crying is just God's way of making our eyes shine. No one ever has to hide their emotions. If you want to stand in the middle of the store or street and cry, do it. If you want to scream, do it. You have to do what is right for you. No one should bottle up their emotions and have the lid burst open when it is least expected.

I want to share some Bible verses that may help you navigate your way through the cloak of grief. Decorate your Bible with sticky notes, as you find the passages for future use. I don't want to speak out of turn here, but I do believe that you will return to them when the time is right for you. Until that day, just keep on doing as you're doing, and everything will follow.

Bible Verses to Help You Navigate Your Grief

- "I can do all this through Him who gives me strength." –Philippians 4:13

- "He will wipe every tear from their eyes. There will be no more death or mourning or crying or pain, for the old order of things has passed away." –Revelation 21:4

- "I consider that our present sufferings are not worth comparing with the glory that will be revealed in us." –Romans 8:18

- "The Lord is close to the brokenhearted and saves those who are crushed in spirit." –Psalms 34:18

- "Come to me, all you who are weary and burdened, and I will give you rest. Take my yoke upon you and learn from me, for I am gentle and humble in heart, and you will find rest for your souls. For my yoke is easy and my burden is light." –Matthew 11:28–30

- "My flesh and my heart may fail, but God is the strength of my heart and my portion forever." —Psalms 73:26

- "Surely he took up our pain and bore our suffering, yet we considered him punished by God, stricken by him, and afflicted. But he was pierced for our transgressions, he was crushed for our iniquities; the punishment that brought us peace was on him, and by his wounds we are healed. We all, like sheep, have gone astray, each of us has turned to our own way; and the Lord has laid on him the iniquity of us all." —Isaiah 53:4–6

These are a handful of the verses that I have found that prove to you, me, and everyone else that God loves you more than you will ever know. He loves us all so much that He sacrificed His Son so that we may be free of sin. The Bible holds so many treasures between the pages. Those treasures are waiting to be discovered by you, me, and everyone—when you are ready. Never doubt that you are loved, and in God's eyes, you are His most perfect creation.

Conclusion

We have reached the part of the book where I take a step back and allow you to take everything you have learned, and apply it to your life and circumstances. I wanted to give you a book that would help you slow down to think about what you have around you. I wanted to present you with the opportunity to stop and listen to the birds, appreciate the beauty of the leaves and branches dancing in the blustering wind, or enjoy the calming effect of the rain as it lands on your window. This book is about more than just words; it is about learning to use your senses to appreciate the gifts that were given to each of us by God. I know that I have successfully passed my intentions to you and everyone who reads this book.

Nature's Reach: Almost the End

Alison and I were visiting Jessica, and we were chatting about life as we know it, which included the news, the pandemic, the financial crisis, and my books. The conversation ended up with us talking about signs from our dearly departed loved ones. We spoke about me finding white feathers in peculiar places, especially in the last couple of months. I knew that Dad was close by because I could feel his presence. At one point, we were getting hungry as it was lunchtime. Alison and I left Jessica and hopped in the car. We decided to go and have a very hearty and healthy lunch at Chick-fil-A, which was four miles away. We continued our conversation about signs on our way over. We stopped at a red light and patiently waited for it to change. During the wait, a white feather landed on the windshield in front of me—on the driver's side! It was right in my line of vision. A rough guess would be that the feather was about two inches long. Did I mention that it was *WHITE*? As suddenly as it appeared, it disappeared again. The initial shock wore off, and Alison and I yelled. We couldn't believe it.

I have been driving for 40 years, and I have never had a feather land on, in, or near my car. We both agreed that Dad was letting me know that he was with me. He wanted to reassure me that he was there to deliver one of the biggest gifts I would ever receive—my first grandchild.

Nature Appreciation

In March of 2020, Alison and I spent a glorious week with Mum and Dad after he had let me know he had been diagnosed with cancer. We spent time talking, watched television, and enjoyed moments of silence. One day, during our visit, the heavens opened up and it poured with rain. This is what a typical day in England looks like. I went outside to see, smell, and hear the rain as it met the grass, trees, and bushes in the garden. I was greeted by the most beautiful sight I had ever seen—a bright rainbow that reached across the garden. I could see where it started and ended, and it was just bright, brilliant, and beautiful. I took it as a sign that there was hope for Dad, but we know what happened. Dad passed away on November 23rd, 2020.

I recently went out and bought dad a birthday card. I started the tradition last year, and I will continue doing it until I join him on his heavenly perch. I wrote a message on the card, signed it, put it in an envelope, filled out the address, placed stamps on the envelope, and dropped it off at the Post Office. Mum will open the card, and place it on the mantle to celebrate his birthday week.

When Alison and I returned home from running some errands, we could hear a thunderstorm building in the distance. We had some pine straw that we needed to spread in the front yard, so we rushed out and did as much as we could before the storm found our home. We hadn't finished spreading the straw when the heavens opened. It was a very angry storm that caused small rivers to form in our yard. The trees were trying to hold onto their roots. Angry flashes of lightning jumped out from the black clouds. I don't think I have experienced that much anger in the weather in a very long time.

As quickly as the storm arrived, it was making a hasty getaway. I grabbed my umbrella and went out into the garden to assess if there had been any damage. Thankfully the damage was minimal and only a couple of branches had broken off. There were leaves everywhere, as well as puddles of water that were trying to seep into the ground. It was still raining, but it was a gentle, soothing rain.

I turned my focus toward the lake, and I could see how the water line had risen from the cloudburst. I turned around to continue assessing my garden, when I got the shock of my life. There was a rainbow in my backyard. I swear it was the same rainbow that I had seen in Mum and Dad's garden two years previously. It spanned across my backyard, and I could see where it started and where it ended, and it had the most vibrant colors. I called Alison to come out and look at it. We stood there in amazement. I walked toward the rainbow to see if it was real. I wanted to touch it. I wanted to stand in it. It looked as if it was coming out of the bench between the trees, over the driveway, and into some bushes in the front yard. We took photos and videos because we wanted to be sure to have evidence when we told others of what we have witnessed.

I had never seen anything like it. Could it have been Dad? I had, after all, just put his birthday card in the mail. Was this his message to say, "I'm here, Son. Thank you." I like to believe that it was him.

The End

Writing this book has been another healing experience for me. I have been blown away by the knowledge I have gained, while doing research and interviewing old and new people. I love that everyone has been open with me, and has shared their opinions and experiences with me. I am blown away by the support I receive from strangers who have read my books, and who have been following along on this journey of healing. It is not an easy journey. I like knowing that I am making a difference in your life. Please consider leaving a review if you have discovered something that helped you find what you were searching for.

<u>*Do Not Stand at My Grave and Weep*</u>

Do not stand by my grave, and weep.

I am not there, I do not sleep-

I am the thousand winds that blow

I am the diamond glints in snow

I am the sunlight on ripened grain,

I am the gentle, autumn rain.

As you awake with morning's hush,

I am the swift up-flinging rush

Of quiet bird in circled flight,

I am the day transcending soft night.

Do not stand by my grave, and cry-

I am not there.

I did not die. –Mary Elizabeth Frye

Until we meet again. Be blessed, and may your God go with you.

References

Ackerman, C. E. (2022, June 20). *83 benefits of journaling for depression, anxiety, and stress.* PositivePsychology.com. https://positivepsychology.com/benefits-of-journaling/

Acquaviva, A. (2014, April 24). *How animals can help, heal and de-stress you.* Utica College. https://www.utica.edu/student-blogs/how-animals-can-help-heal-and-de-stress-you/

Admin. (2020, July 5). *5 ways the weather can affect your mental health.* Enlightened Solutions. https://enlightenedsolutions.com/5-ways-the-weather-can-affect-your-mental-health/

Aimee. (2022, July 14). *25 excellent benefits of reading the bible daily.* Mama Reflections. https://mamareflections.com/25-excellent-benefits-of-reading-the-bible-daily/

Albert. (2021, March 15). *Health benefits of fishing: Good for body and mind.* FishingBooker. https://fishingbooker.com/blog/health-benefits-of-fishing/

Andrea. (2018, January 21). *How horses can help you deal with grief.* Withers Whisper. https://witherswhisper.com/equine-gestalt/

Beaton, P. (2015, February 26). *Surprising ways the weather affects your well-being.* Expertrain. https://www.expertrain.com/blog/happiness/how-weather-affects-wellbeing.htm

The BibleStudyTools Staff. (2021, November 16). *Bible verses about grief.* Bible Study Tools. https://www.biblestudytools.com/topical-verses/bible-verses-for-overcoming-grief/

Bolster, M. (2019, June 6). *How to manage grief through journaling.* Brain and Life. https://www.brainandlife.org/the-magazine/online-exclusives/how-to-manage-grief-through-journaling/

Brennan, D. (2021, October 25). *Mental health benefits of the beach.* WebMD. https://www.webmd.com/mental-health/mental-health-benefits-of-the-beach

Cemetery visits provide healing and grief therapy. (2010, May 26). iMortuary. https://www.imortuary.com/blog/cemetery-visits-provide-healing-and-grief-therapy/

Clifton-Ross, J. (2021, May 14). *5 ways insects make our world a better place.* Nature Conservancy of Canada (NCC). https://www.natureconservancy.ca/en/blog/5-ways-insects-make-our-world.html#.Yv5QSRxBzIU

Crimmins, A., Balbus, J., Gamble, J. L., Beard, C. B., Bell, J. E., Dodgen, D., Eisen, R. J., Fann, N., Hawkins, M. D., Herring, S. C., Jantarasami, L., Mills, D. M., Saha, S., Sarofim, M. C., Trtanj, J., & Ziska, L. (2016). *The impacts of climate change on human health in the United States: A scientific assessment.* U.S. Global Change Research Program. https://doi.org/10.7930/j0r49nqx

Davis, H. (2021, June 1). *How spending time traveling can help with grief.* Go Backpacking. https://gobackpacking.com/how-traveling-can-help-with-grief/

Davis, S. (2021, June 26). *How does reading the Bible affect your brain, according to the experts.* Susan L Davis. https://www.susanldavis.com/how-does-reading-the-bible-affect-your-brain/

Dresden, D. (2020, November 3). *What to know about the health benefits of sunlight?* MedicalNewsToday. https://www.medicalnewstoday.com/articles/benefits-of-sunlight

Dunkle, F. (2012, April 17). *The Bible and the brain.* United Church of God. https://www.ucg.org/vertical-thought/the-bible-and-the-brain

Eatough, E. (2021, December 13). *You have more than 5 human senses. How are you using yours?* BetterUp. https://www.betterup.com/blog/human-senses

Fane, B. (2016, January 13). *Grief symptoms: How grief affects the brain.* Barbara Fane, LCSW, BCD. https://barbarafane.com/grief-symptoms-how-grief-affects-the-brain/

Faust, P. (2019, June 20). *Does weather influence our brain?* My Boomer Brain. https://www.myboomerbrain.com/post/does-weather-influence-our-brain

Ferguson, M. A., Nielsen, J. A., King, J. B., Dai, L., Giangrasso, D. M., Holman, R., Korenberg, J. R., & Anderson, J. S. (2018) Reward, salience, and attentional networks are activated by religious experience in devout Mormons. *Social Neuroscience, 13*(1), 104-116. https://www.tandfonline.com/doi/10.1080/17470919.2016.1257437

Feyrecilde, M., & Buzhardt, L. (n.d.). *Factors to consider in pet selection—Dogs.* VCA Animal Hospitals. https://vcahospitals.com/know-your-pet/factors-to-consider-in-pet-selection---dogs

Field, B. (2022, April 3). *How weather changes can affect your mental health.* Verywell Mind. https://www.verywellmind.com/how-weather-changes-can-affect-your-mental-health-5222029

Foster, J. (2022, February 25). *Examples of highly successful people who journal.* Createwritenow.com. https://www.createwritenow.com/journal-writing-blog/examples-of-highly-successful-people-who-journal

Fowler, K. (2018, September 27). *The calming effect of therapy chickens.* Next Avenue. https://www.nextavenue.org/calming-effect-therapy-chickens/

Frye, M. E. (1932) *Do not stand at my grave and weep.* Aftering. http://www.aftering.com/top-10-poems-1-do-not-stand/

Green, C. (2019, July 9). *Why going for a retreat in the mountains is best for your mental health?* Wanderlands.

https://wanderlands.org/why-going-for-a-retreat-in-the-mountains-is-best-for-your-mental-health/

Gregoire, C. (2017, December 6). *The surprising ways the weather affects your health and well-being.* HuffPost Canada; HuffPost. https://www.huffpost.com/entry/climate-health_n_4568505

Harvard Health Publishing. (2016, November 15). *Writing to ease grief and loss.* https://www.health.harvard.edu/mind-and-mood/writing-to-ease-grief

Healing your brain after loss: How grief rewires the brain. (2021, September 29). American Brain Foundation. https://www.americanbrainfoundation.org/how-tragedy-affects-the-brain/

Hefton, A. (2021, June 29). *Grief in the Bible: Helping you cope in times of trouble.* Seattle Christian Counseling. https://seattlechristiancounseling.com/articles/grief-in-the-bible-helping-you-cope-in-times-of-trouble

Hone, L. (2020, February 19). *What I learned about resilience in the midst of grief.* Greater Good. https://greatergood.berkeley.edu/article/item/what_i_learned_about_resilience_in_the_midst_of_grief

How to attract wildlife to your garden. (2022, February 11). Gardening Is Great. https://gardeningisgreat.com/how-to-attract-wildlife-to-your-garden/

John Hopkins Medicine. (2021, July 14). *Brain anatomy and how the brain works.*

https://www.hopkinsmedicine.org/health/conditions-and-diseases/anatomy-of-the-brain

John Ruskin Quotes. (n.d.). BrainyQuote. https://www.brainyquote.com/quotes/john_ruskin_108460?src=t_weather

Kay, F. (2021, July 27). *Do animals experience grief?* Everlasting Memories. https://www.evrmemories.com/do-animals-experience-grief

Kessler, C. (2022, January 21). *5 benefits of a grief journal.* Funeral Basics. https://www.funeralbasics.org/benefits-grief-journal/

Kravits, S. L. (2017, April 25). *Grief and weather.* Lifewithoutjudgment. https://www.lifewithoutjudgment.com/single-post/2017/04/25/Grief-and-weather

Kwik Learning. (2021, March 19). *How cold weather affects the brain.*https://kwiklearning.com/kwik-tips/how-cold-weather-affects-the-brain/

Loza, B. (2019, May 20). *Unsung heroes: 10 ways animals help us.* GlobalGiving. https://www.globalgiving.org/learn/ways-animals-help-us/

Mayo Clinic Staff. (2021, December 14). *Seasonal affective disorder (SAD).* Mayo Clinic. https://www.mayoclinic.org/diseases-conditions/seasonal-affective-disorder/symptoms-causes/syc-20364651

McCoy, B. (2021, December 20). How your brain copes with grief, and why it takes time to heal. *NPR*. https://www.npr.org/sections/health-shots/2021/12/20/1056741090/grief-loss-holiday-brain-healing

Mendoza, M. A. (2021, January 26). *How journaling can help you grieve*. Psychology Today. https://www.psychologytoday.com/us/blog/understanding-grief/202101/how-journaling-can-help-you-grieve

Miles, L. (2020, February 21). *Brain and emotions: How anger, fear, or love work in your brain*. Learning Mind. https://www.learning-mind.com/brain-and-emotions/

Mills, A. (2018, September 2). *The most fascinating animal senses in the world*. AnimalWised. https://www.animalwised.com/the-most-fascinating-animal-senses-in-the-world-2635.html

Mountain, V. (2021, August 21). *Coping with grief and loss: How Christians and churches can help*. Stirling College. https://stirling.edu.au/grief/

New International Version. (n.d.). BibleGateway.com. https://www.biblegateway.com/versions/New-International-Version-NIV-Bible/

Nowinski, J., & Jeffries, A. (2016, June 18). *Healing horses: Equine therapy for grieving children*. Psychology Today. https://www.psychologytoday.com/us/blog/the-almost-effect/201606/healing-horses-equine-therapy-grieving-children

NRCS. (2020). *Plants & Animals*. USDA. https://www.nrcs.usda.gov/wps/portal/nrcs/main/national/plantsanimals/

Park, A. (2017, August 7). *Why sunlight is so good for you*. Time. https://time.com/4888327/why-sunlight-is-so-good-for-you/

Raymond, C. (2022, February 15). *How to cope with the physical effects of grief*. Verywell Mind. https://www.verywellmind.com/physical-symptoms-of-grief-4065135

Seppälä, E. (2017, July 11). *How animals heal us and teach us*. Psychology Today. https://www.psychologytoday.com/us/blog/feeling-it/201707/how-animals-heal-us-and-teach-us

Smith, A. (2018, January 30). *The essential guide to rats*. Ehrlich Pest Control. https://www.jcehrlich.com/blog/the-essential-guide-to-rats

Stang, H. (2021, May 27). *Grief journaling tips & writing prompts*. Mindfulness & Grief Institute. https://mindfulnessandgrief.com/grief-journaling/

Steber, C. (2016, August 12). *11 things to consider before getting a pet*. Bustle. https://www.bustle.com/articles/176279-11-things-to-consider-before-getting-a-pet-because-its-a-huge-responsibility

Trafton, A. (2016, March 31). *How the brain processes emotions*. Massachusetts Institute of Technology. https://news.mit.edu/2016/brain-processes-emotions-mental-illness-depression-0331

Waichler, I. (2022, September 9). *Grief brain: What it is, symptoms, & how to cope.* Choosing Therapy. https://www.choosingtherapy.com/grief-brain/

Wallace, R. (2021, September 3). *Health benefits of fishing: 13 positive physical and mental effects.* Tackle Village. https://tacklevillage.com/health-benefits-of-fishing-13-positive-physical-and-mental-effects/

Weaver II, E. A., & Doyle, H. H. (2019, August 11). *How does the brain work.* Dana Foundation. https://www.dana.org/article/how-does-the-brain-work/

Weir, K. (2020, April 1). Nurtured by nature. *American Psychological Association.* https://www.apa.org/monitor/2020/04/nurtured-nature

White-Lewis, S. (2019). Equine-assisted therapies using horses as healers: A concept analysis. *Nursing Open, 7*(1), 58–67. https://doi.org/10.1002/nop2.377

Why does rain make you feel relaxed? (n.d.). Willspost. https://willspost.com/why-does-rain-make-you-feel-relaxed/

Williams, J., Shorter, G. W., Howlett, N., Zakrzewski-Fruer, J., & Chater, A. M. (2021). Can physical activity support grief outcomes in individuals who have been bereaved? A systematic review. *Sports Medicine—Open, 7*(1), NA–NA. https://doi.org/10.1186/s40798-021-00311-z

Wolfe, S. (2022, July 11). *5 artists whose diaries are as inspiring as their art.* Artland Magazine.

https://magazine.artland.com/5-artists-whose-diaries-are-as-inspiring-as-their-art/

Wood, L. (n.d.). *Grief travel: How & why vacations can help heal your grief.* Eterneva. https://eterneva.com/blog/traveling-while-grieving/

Young, M. (2020, January 19). *How to attract beneficial wildlife to the home garden.* Farm Fit Living. https://farmfitliving.com/how-to-attract-beneficial-wildlife-to-the-home-garden/

Zelenski, J. M., & Nisbet, E. K. (2012). Happiness and feeling connected: The distinct role of nature relatedness. *Environment and Behavior, 46*(1), 3–23. https://doi.org/10.1177/0013916512451901

Image References

Allen, J. (2022a, August 30). *4 types of animals* [Image]. John Allen.

Allen, J. (2022b, August 30). *Rainbow* [Image]. John Allen.

Allen, J. (2022c, August 30). *Samantha up close* [Image]. John Allen.

Bowers, J. (2018, January 25). *[Brown grass field towards trees]* [Image]. Unsplash. https://unsplash.com/photos/BqKdvJ8a5TI

Burden, A. (2017, June 16). *[Open book]* [Image]. Unsplash. https://unsplash.com/photos/TNlHf4m4gpI

Fakurian, M. (2021, April 7). *[Blue and green peacock feather]* [Image]. Unsplash. https://unsplash.com/photos/58Z17lnVS4U

Miriam G. (2021, July 2). *[Matthew 11:28 note]* [Image]. Unsplash. https://unsplash.com/photos/duDxwYT9GPU

Glas, J. (2018, March 14). *[Curved concrete road beside grass]* [Image]. Unsplash. https://unsplash.com/photos/P6iOpqQpwwU

Grossgasteiger, E. (2018, August 14). *[Three assorted-color horses standing on green grass]* [Image]. Unsplash. https://unsplash.com/photos/38_XHFO6ycI

Hiles, G. (2018, December 29). *[Flowers near beach]* [Image]. Unsplash. https://unsplash.com/photos/p8OqXnGGNcE

Hudson, D. (2018, February 24). *[Cathedral interior]* [Image]. Unsplash. https://unsplash.com/photos/sgdyBq6kheQ

Macháček, Z. (2020, May 11). *[Green and brown humming bird]* [Image]. Unsplash. https://unsplash.com/photos/RiM-wOomC6w

Millar, S. (2020, August 22). *[Pink and white flowers on gray concrete tomb]* [Image]. Unsplash. https://unsplash.com/photos/cQ-66Evaf5g

Pastourmatzis, P. (2018, July 19). *[Person attempting to grab feather floating beside water]* [Image]. Unsplash. https://unsplash.com/photos/Vs_zkj1sEHc

Ponzi, C. (2019, January 8). *[Deer on hill in forest]* [Image]. Unsplash. https://unsplash.com/photos/8fPAgCoAY_E

Poulin, A. (2016, May 25). *Sunset picnic* [Image]. Unsplash. https://unsplash.com/photos/NhU0nUR7920

Tran, T. (2017, October 4). Sunshine lovers [Image]. Unsplash. https://unsplash.com/photos/ygQ0nN4y11k

WanderLabs. (2019, February 11). *[Person holding I haven't been everywhere but it's on my list card]* [Image]. Unsplash. https://unsplash.com/photos/vKTxINZcvbE

Weber, S. (2021, July 2). *Coffee mug next to a journal with dead roses on a wooden background* [Image]. Unsplash. https://unsplash.com/photos/xcWd06vcsJo

Wolff, C. (2018, March 14). *[Person crying beside bed]* [Image]. Unsplash. https://unsplash.com/photos/owBcefxgrIE

Printed in Great Britain
by Amazon

21674892R00082